More than Luck

Surviving World War II and Communist Deportation in Hungary (1943–1959)

Dear Sonia,
You are Number One!
Thank you for the
font size change!

Maria
12-18-16

More than Luck

Surviving World War II and Communist Deportation in Hungary (1943–1959)

Maria Csonka Bardos

SHIRES PRESS
4869 Main Street | Manchester Center, VT 05255
www.northshire.com

More than Luck
Surviving World War II and Communist Deportation in Hungary (1943–1959)

ISBN: 978-1-60571-314-4
Library of Congress Number: 2016950371

Cover photographs: Top, pre-World War II Elizabeth Bridge; Bottom, Hungarian Parliament Building

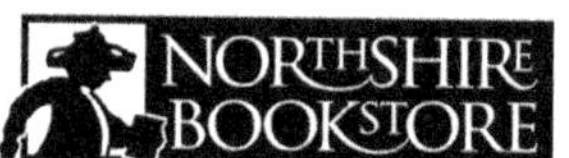

Building Community, One Book at a Time
A family-owned, independent bookstore in Manchester Ctr., VT, since 1976 and Saratoga Springs, NY since 2013.
We are committed to excellence in bookselling.
The Northshire Bookstore's mission is to serve as a resource for information, ideas, and entertainment while honoring the needs of customers, staff, and community.

Printed in the United States of America

For

Susan Antonia Csonka

Preface

Much of my family's survival of the horrors of World War II truly depended on "pure luck." That is, being in the right place at the right time, particularly when bullets and bombs were falling.

But besides pure luck, it was also "hard work" that helped my family to endure for nine weeks in a fallout shelter. Quick adaptability to changing conditions helped the Csonka families avoid foreseeable disasters.

Pure luck characterized our years of deportation (1951–53). We could have been sent to a less accommodating town than Mezőberény, where helpful neighbors and field work opportunities changed us forever. But, yes, it took hard work on the part of my family of city dwellers to get used to the agricultural environment into which we were placed by force. And it took hard work to adapt to the loneliness of our day-to-day existence without our extended family. Only the death of Stalin in 1953 liberated my mother, my siblings, and me from the nightmare of a possible relocation to Siberia.

Luck and hard work, yes, but also fortitude, perseverance, and unstinting love. My mother was the supreme example of these characteristics that made it possible for us to survive the war and deportation, and the additional years until we became a united family again.

Contents

Introduction

My life is like a large, colorful patchwork quilt. In it, I can see squares, little vignettes that represent the most memorable episodes of my life.

In one corner, I see myself as a three-year-old in Balatonszemes, Hungary, saying "Good morning, madame" to the cow in the stable to which my father took me to get our fresh milk for the day.

In another corner I am in Mátrafüred in northern Hungary; there, I see myself stealing the maypole from a cordoned-off area where my brother John and two older male cousins posted a "no girls allowed" sign.

On still another patch, at the top of a black walnut tree, I see myself in a tree house, which my male cousins built for all who dared to climb up high.

Still in another corner, I see myself in Mezőberény in eastern Hungary, trying to tear my hair out as I study Russian on my own, with the hope that I could pass the first-year Russian exam in Budapest.

The quilt has happy and sad spots in it. One of the saddest moments in my ten-year-old life is not being able to say "good-bye" to my father, who had to flee Budapest in May 1948.

The vignettes multiply and multiply. In Budapest in the winter of 1958 I see myself at age twenty, giving a party in our home with sandwiches and dancing to "capitalist" music. I am five-feet six-inches tall and slender, wearing a three-tier black taffeta gown, which my father sent me from Buffalo, New York.

And, in the middle of the quilt, I see myself, with outstretched arms, as I finally say "hello" to my father at Idlewild Airport, New York, U.S.A., on June 16, 1959. I had not seen him in eleven years.

Maria Csonka Bardos
January 2016

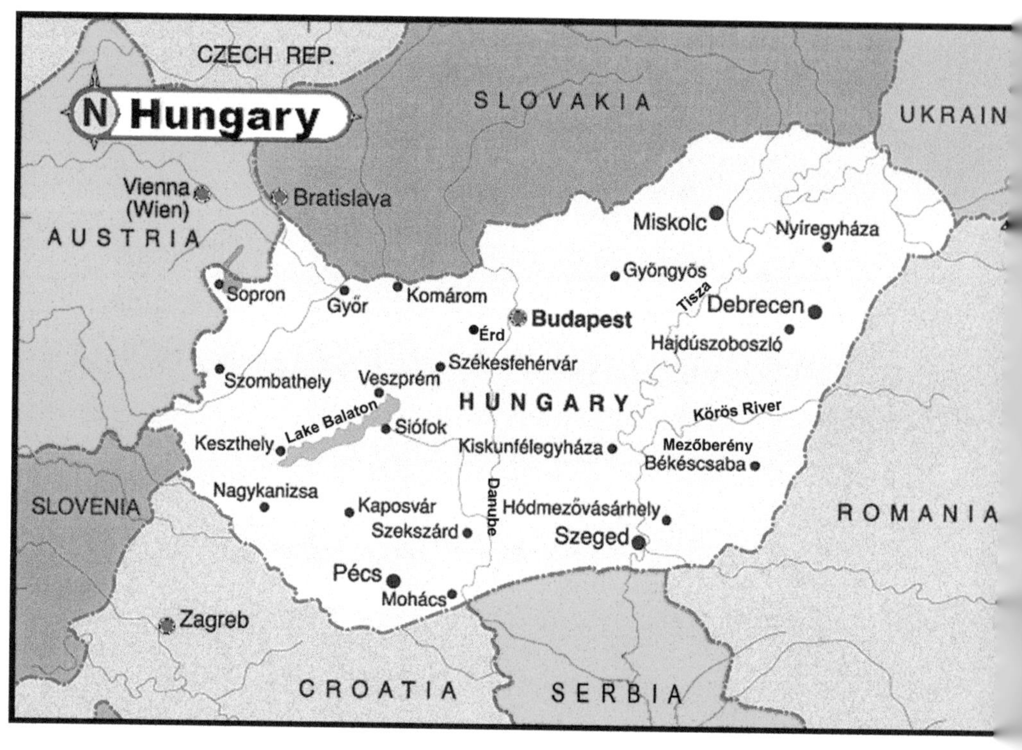
Hungary
N
CZECH REP.
SLOVAKIA
UKRAIN
Vienna (Wien)
Bratislava
AUSTRIA
Miskolc
Nyíregyháza
Gyöngyös
Sopron
Győr
Komárom
Budapest
Tisza
Debrecen
Érd
Hajdúszoboszló
Szombathely
Veszprém
Székesfehérvár
HUNGARY
Lake Balaton
Siófok
Körös River
Keszthely
Kiskunfélegyháza
Mezőberény
Békéscsaba
SLOVENIA
Nagykanizsa
Kaposvár
Danube
Hódmezővásárhely
ROMANIA
Szekszárd
Szeged
Pécs
Mohács
Zagreb
CROATIA
SERBIA

PART I

Family

Grandfather János Csonka, Inventor

Once upon a time there was a Hungarian inventor by the name of János Csonka, and he was my grandfather. He was born in 1852 in Szeged, Hungary, the seventh child of a blacksmith, Vince Tsonka. Working side by side with his father, young János Csonka learned important skills in iron working that helped him in later life to build automobiles.

Grandfather never finished elementary school. But he had an inquisitive mind and a great desire to see the world. He went to places where he could learn about the most up-to-date technological inventions of the day. In Paris, he studied the sewing machine industry, and in England, he mastered the technology of the steam engine. The main interest of my grandfather was the field of internal combustion.

At the age of twenty-five, in 1877, Grandfather returned to Hungary. He was appointed the workshop leader of the newly formed Technical University of Budapest. There, for the next forty-eight years, he taught future generations of Hungarian engineers.

In 1891, my grandfather, together with his friend and co-worker Donát Bánki, invented the "Bánki-Csonka carburetor." This was a brilliant invention in which gasoline, a highly combustible product, was vaporized and regulated with a butterfly valve. This invention, patented in February 1893, made Donát Bánki and János Csonka world famous.

Some years later in 1905 my grandfather used the technology of carburation to build a fleet of automobiles for the Hungarian Postal Department. These cars are noteworthy because they were the pioneers of the Hungarian auto manufacturing industry.

János Csonka became a highly revered figure in the field of Hungarian engineering. At his retirement at age seventy-three in 1925, he received the honorary title of "Engineer" from the Hungarian Chamber of Engineers. The chamber invoked the "genius" clause when conferring this honor on him.

During World War I, Grandfather bought a large apartment house in a very elegant section of Buda, at Horthy Miklós Street 31. It had three stories and a total of twenty commodious apartments, with a full basement. When he retired, he founded a small machine shop in the basement of his building. There he worked with thirteen employees, among them his two sons, John Csonka and Béla Csonka. Out of this small establishment grew the Csonka Machine Factory, which in 1941 employed more than one thousand workers. My father, John Csonka, and my uncle, Béla Csonka, were the co-directors of the plant.

Grandfather died in 1939, at the age of eighty-nine. His energy and creativity became legendary for generations of Hungarian engineers who knew him. János Csonka was a role model for his grandchildren, although only six of us had been born at the time of death. Nevertheless, all eleven living Csonka grandchildren were brought up with the knowledge of his genius.

The Three Csonka Brothers

Grandfather married late in life at the age of forty-three in 1895. His bride, Johanna (Jenny) Winkler, from Arad, Transylvania, was twenty-nine. They lived in Budapest and had five children: two daughters and three sons.

They named their daughters Ilona and Mária. The older daughter, Ilona (born 1898), was the third child born to János and Jenny. Ilona married János Feyér, had a child in 1927 called Iluska, and died at the age of forty. Iluska, being the first of twelve Csonka grandchildren, enjoyed the status of "first and only" until cousin Paul was born eight years later. Sadly, Iluska died of pneumonia in 1939, one year after her mother's death. Mária (born 1901) was the second daughter of my grandparents, their youngest child, and my namesake; she never married and died in her ninety-fourth year.

My grandparents' three sons were named Pál, János, and Béla. All of the sons inherited their father's technical interests. The oldest son, Paul (born 1896), became a prominent architect and a professor of structural mechanics (statics) at the Technical University of Budapest. According to documents discovered later, the Hungarian Communist Party considered him to be "the most dangerous" professor at this university. Nevertheless, in 1954 he received the coveted Kossuth Prize from the Hungarian government for his outstanding contributions.

After receiving their technical training in the workshop of my grandfather, both the second son, John (born 1897), and the third son, Béla (born 1900), graduated as mechanical engineers from the university's department of engineering. These younger Csonka brothers established a working environment in their factory that became legendary for its humanitarian concern, which the owners displayed toward every one of their employees.

The three brothers had many remarkable parallels in their lives. They each married in the mid-1930s, and each moved with his young wife to my grandfather's apartment house. Two of the young wives, Nelli and Margó, were thirteen years younger than their husbands and knew each other well, having been schoolmates for eight years.

My father, John Csonka, and his wife, my mother, Kornélia (Nelli) Simon, lived on the third floor of the building in a beautiful sunny apartment. Immediately below, on the second floor, Uncle Paul resided with his wife, Margó Warga, and on the first floor below them lived Uncle Béla with his wife, Ili Wotzasik.

Some curious parallels continued in the families of the Csonka brothers. By coincidence, the first-born child in each family was a boy. These boys were remarkably close in age: Paul Jr. (born 1935), John Jr. (born 1935), and Béla Jr. (born 1937). After a three-year period, each family had a daughter. These girls were born, likewise, very close in age, all in 1938. Maria, Melinda, and Margit—always called Mazsi, but first by her father as she was his little raisin (*mazsola*). Then, three years later in the 1940s, three more daughters were born: Lívia (born 1940), Judy (born 1941), and Lilla (born 1942). The parallels in the sexes and ages of the Csonka children continued even after World War II. Géza Csonka was born in 1946 and László (Laci) Csonka was born in 1947.

We were very lucky because we all lived in the same apartment building and always found somebody who was ready for a sleepover. The three boys were always playing war games, the three older girls were baking together, and the three younger girls were playing with their stuffed animals.

The person who was overjoyed by having so many children in the family was my widowed grandmother,

"Jenny Mama" Csonka. She lived on the first floor of my grandfather's apartment building starting in 1946 and gave many parties: now, for the three older boys; other times, for the three older girls; and then, in turn, for the three younger girls. And, baby Géza received his share of her love and affection. My younger brother Laci was born the year after she died.

Grandmother Csonka was a great gardener and fantastic cook. With her unmarried daughter, Aunt Mária, she rose every morning at five o'clock and began organizing the meal for the day. She baked the most delicious almond crescents as treats for her grandchildren. And even when Jenny Mama died at age eighty-two in December 1946, she was found kneading bread in the kitchen.

But, our simple, harmonious lives were brutally interrupted by the events of World War II. The one and only goal of the Csonka brothers was to protect their families—their mother, their wives, and the nine Csonka grandchildren (born in the years 1935-42)—from the horrors of the political events that reached into our everyday lives and destroyed our feeling of security. The three brothers' struggle to stay alive during these difficult times is the subject of the second chapter of my book.

My Family and Religion

I come from a Roman Catholic family background. During my younger years, my parents took my siblings and me to Sunday services on a regular basis. Most of the year we attended the beautiful neo-Baroque parish church named after Hungary's Saint Emery, patron of the Eleventh District of Budapest, where most of the Catholics resided. In the winter we went to a grotto chapel on the side of Gellért Hill overlooking the Danube, which we called the "church in the cave" (*Sziklakápolna*). During the war years (1943–45) religion and spirituality played a crucially significant role in my family. Only their faith in God helped many of my relatives during the apparently hopeless situations that were occurring before, during, and after the siege of Budapest.

With the emergence of the Communist Party in 1946, being "religiously oriented" became an automatic, open protest against the Marxist system. As co-chairs of the Catholic Parish Council in our district, my father and Aunt Margó openly gave their support to the leader of the Catholic Church in Hungary, Cardinal József Mindszenty, chief opponent of the communist ideology and an organizer of the Hungarian resistance.

In spring 1948, the Communist Party dissolved all religious orders in Hungary. Although people were still allowed to go to church, any public demonstration of one's faith was forbidden. I was a teenager in this nonreligious atmosphere. Students were discouraged from talking about religious matters in school. Yet, secretly, my sister and I were receiving private religious instruction from a priest, a friend of the family, whom we supported with food donations.

As I look back, I realize my initial religious upbringing gave me a solid foundation during my elementary-school years. And later, my spiritual upbringing helped me to face up to some of the most difficult situations that my young life presented in a Communist country.

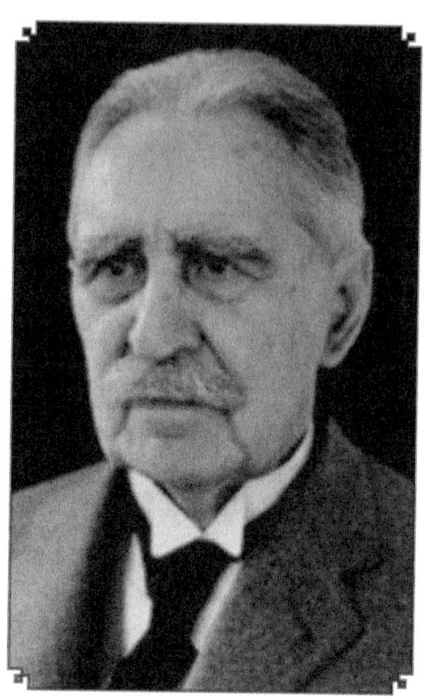

Grandfather János Csonka, age 82

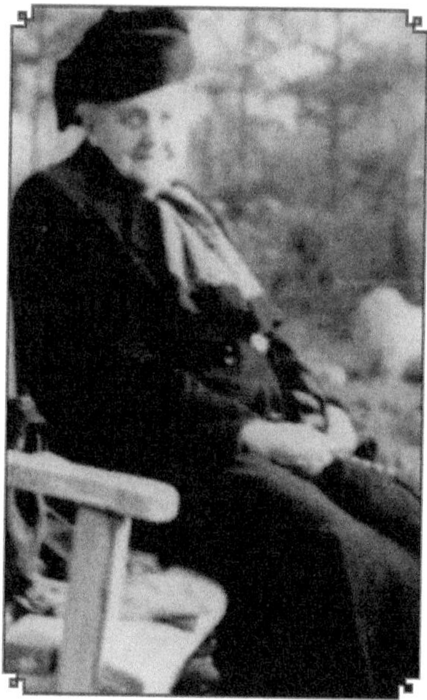

Grandmother Jenny Csonka, age 80

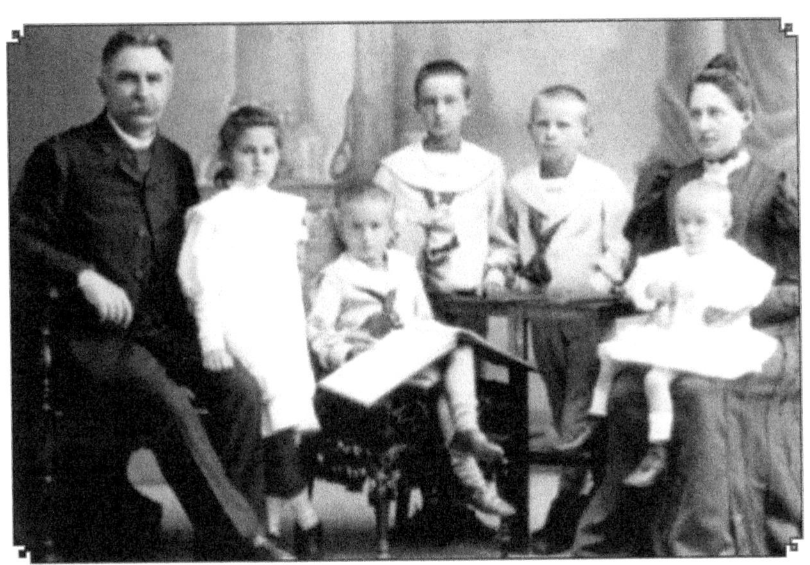

János and Jenny Winkler Csonka with their five children. From left: Ilona, Béla, Paul, John, Mária. Budapest, 1903

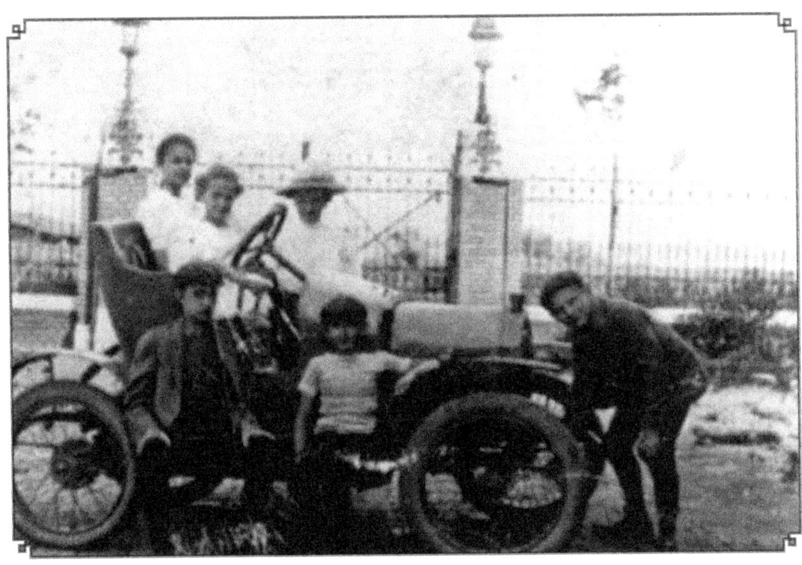

Csonka children with their father's car. From left, top: Ilona, Maria, babysitter; below: Paul, Béla, John. Budapest, 1909

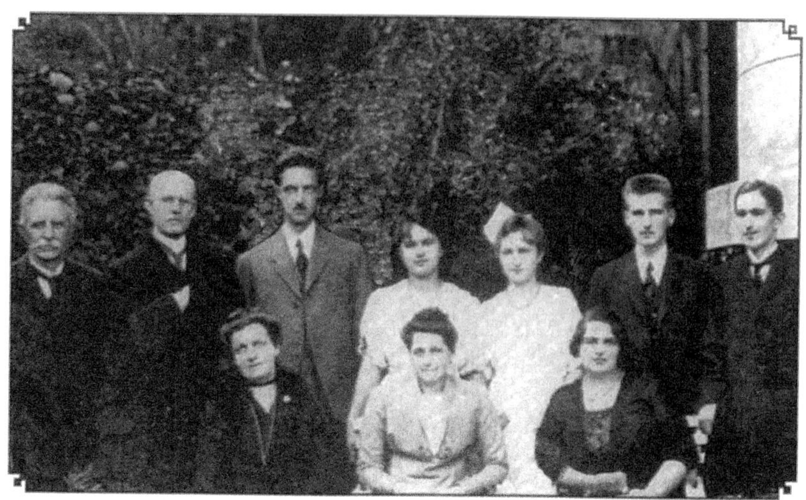

Csonkas and Winklers. Top row, from left: János Csonka; Anton Hochenburger (husband of Emilia Winkler); son Paul; daughters Ilona and Mária; sons John and Béla; seated, from left: Ella (wife of Louis Winkler); Jenny Winkler Csonka; Vilma Boross-Pastwa (half sister of Jenny). c. 1919

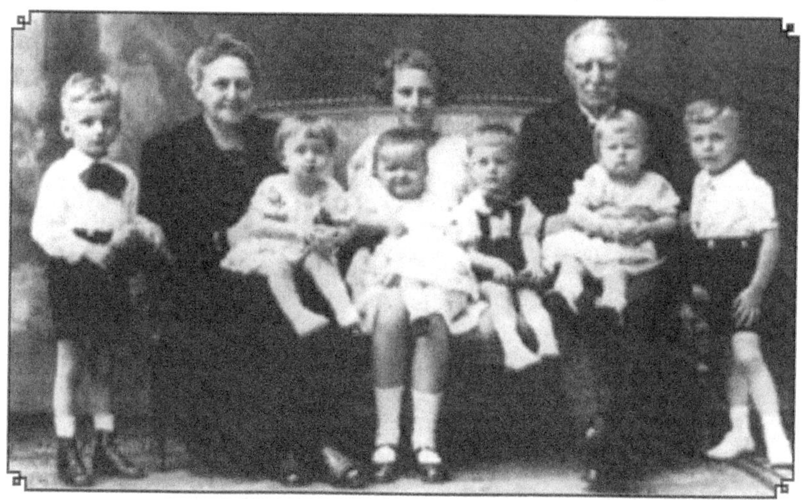

Csonka grandchildren. From left: Paul Jr., Grandmother Csonka holding Mazsi, Iluska holding Melinda, Béla Jr., Grandfather Csonka holding Maria, John Jr. Budapest, 1939

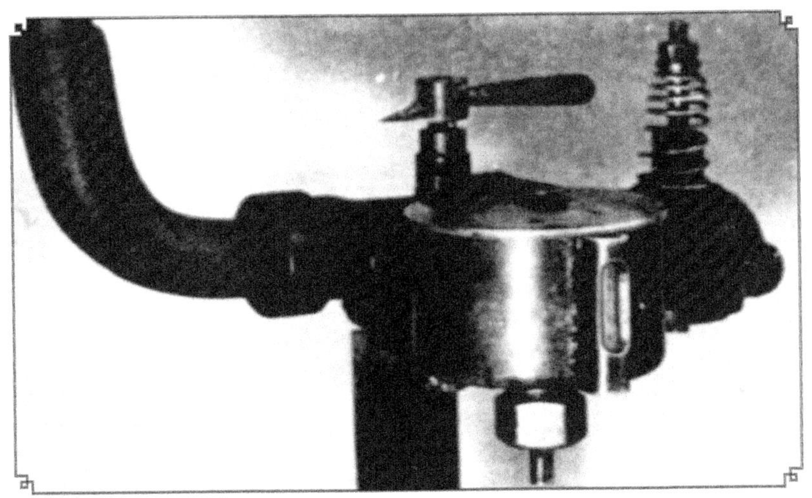

Bánki-Csonka carburetor. The first atomizing carburetor was co-invented by János Csonka and Donát Bánki in 1891. The Hungarian patent was issued on February 11, 1893. The first model is preserved at the national Museum of Science and Technology in Budapest and was on display at the 1958 World's Fair in Brussels. The inventors gave it the name porlasztó *meaning atomizer.*

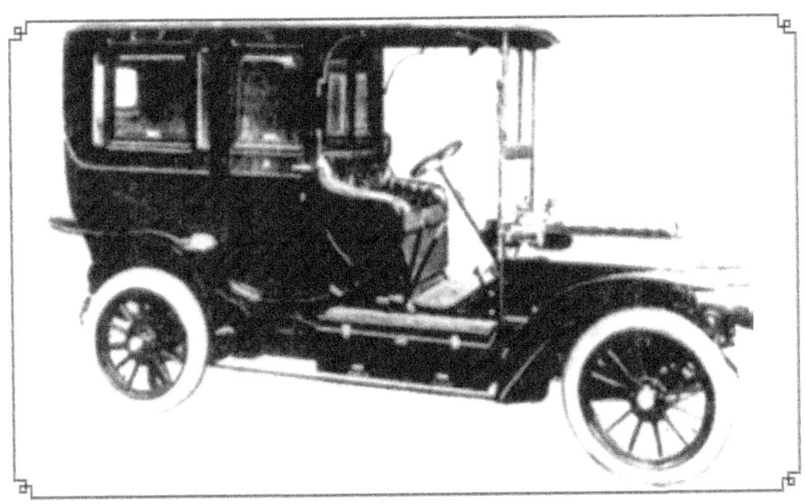

Grandfather's one-cylinder, four-horsepower car. 1901

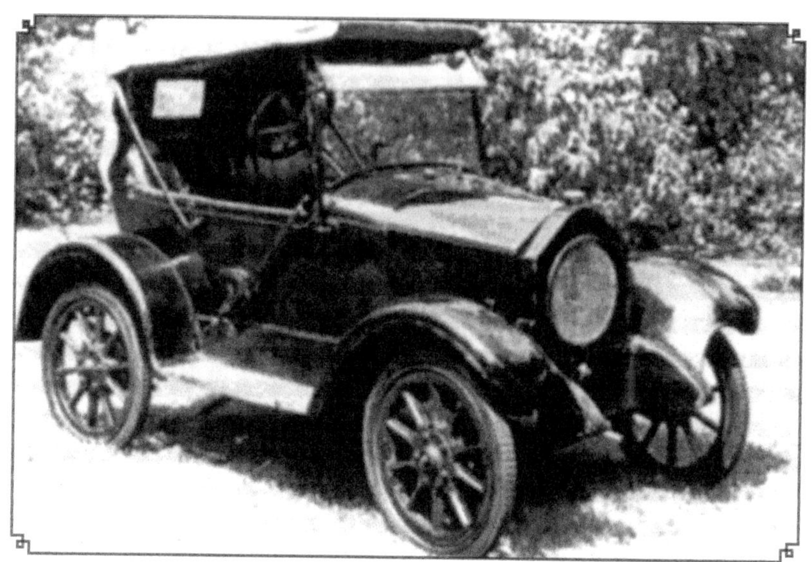

Grandfather's four-cylinder, twenty-five horsepower car.
1908

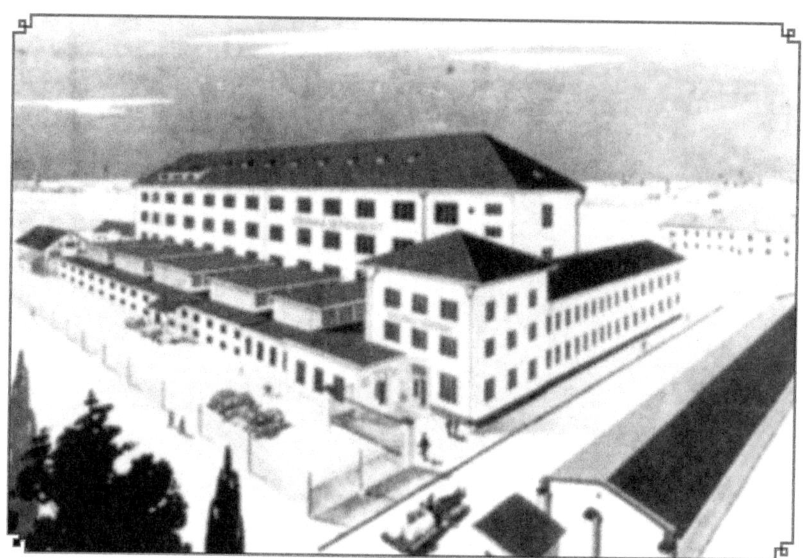

Csonka Machine Factory. Budapest, 1943

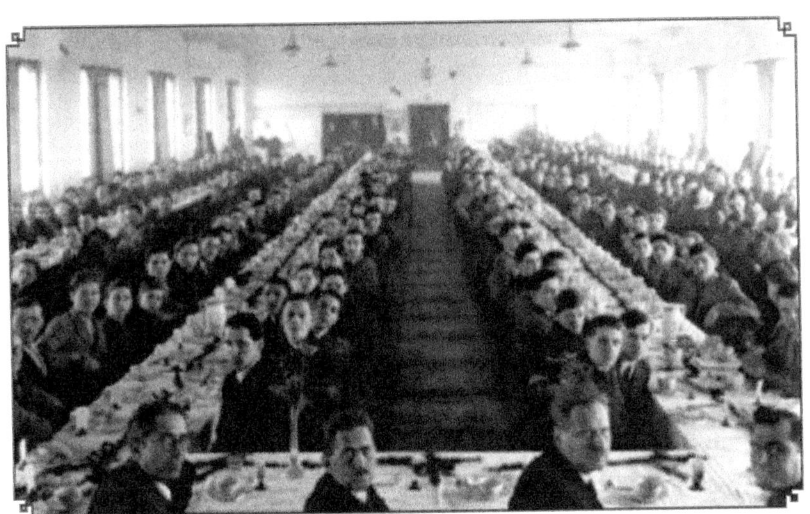

Management dinner at the Csonka factory. In foreground, seated in the middle: co-owners Béla Csonka and John Csonka. 1942

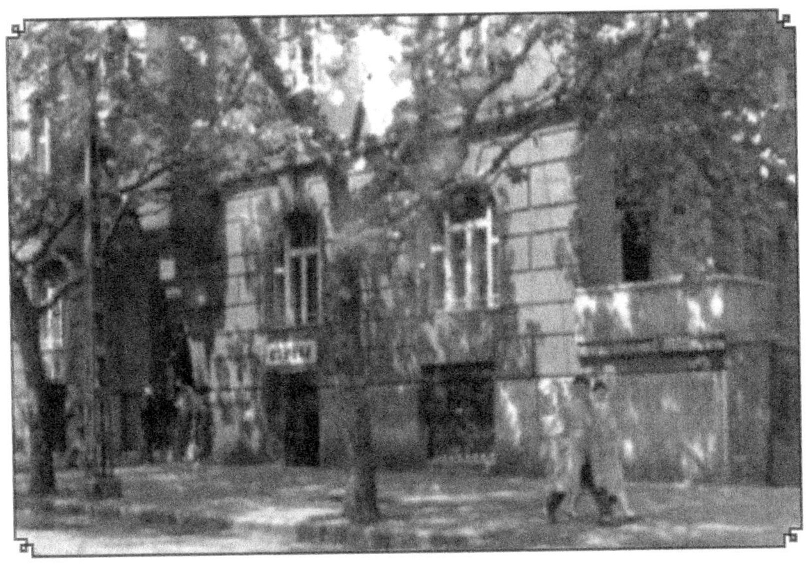

Grandfather's apartment building at Béla Bartók Street 31 (previously Horthy Miklós Street). His three sons – Paul, John, and Béla – and their families lived on different floors. There were twenty apartments in all.

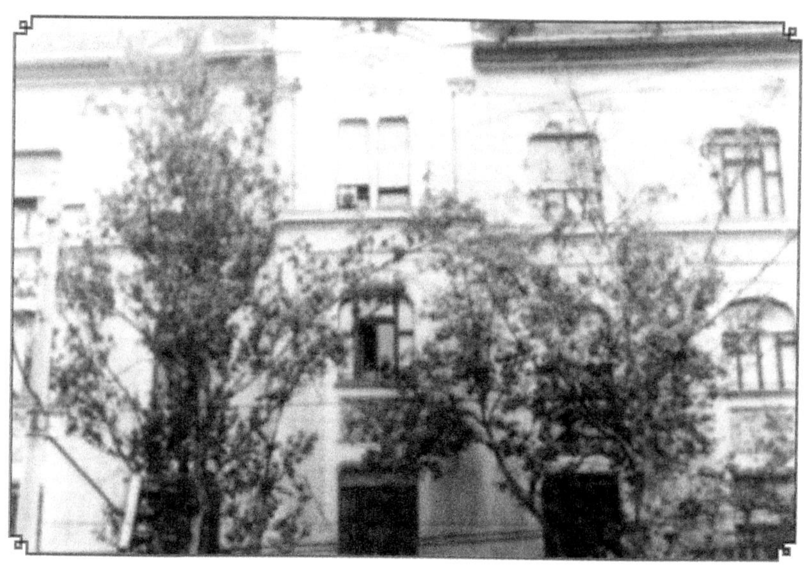

John and Nelli Csonka and their four children lived on the top sunny floor of Grandfather's building.

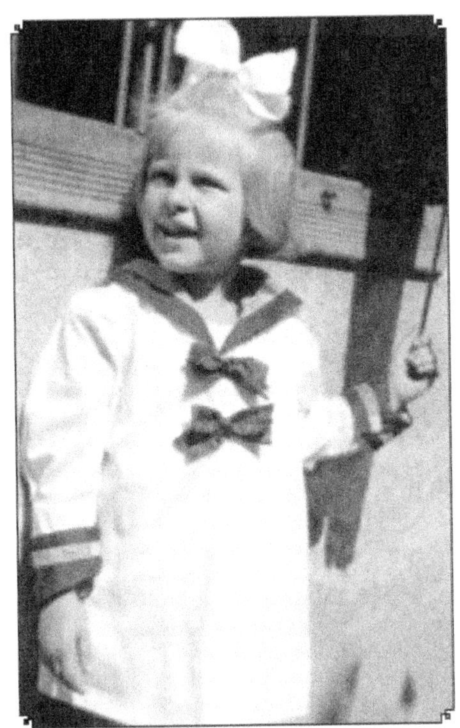

Maria Csonka. 1941

PART II

The War Years

(1943-1945)

From Lake Balaton to Budapest

Nine of the Csonka grandchildren—Paul, John, Béla, Maria, Mazsi, Melinda, Lívia, Judy, and Lilla—grew up at a time when the Nazi regime brought nothing but fear into the hearts of the Hungarian people. In a way, we grew up too fast during the war years. Although we were playful and carefree on the surface, we knew, in the depths of our awareness, that something horrible was going to happen in our lives.

Our fathers had established a comfortable upper-middle-class environment for their families. We were wealthy, but none of us flaunted our wealth. The children in each family were brought up with a German-speaking nanny because our parents realized how important the knowledge of the German language would be in terms of Hungary's political and geographical situations.

The nine of us spent our summers on Lake Balaton, the largest lake of Central Europe, in Hungary's famous resort area. Uncle Paul and Aunt Margó bought a magnificent villa in a beautiful garden in Balatonszemes, on the southern shore of the lake in 1938. My own parents bought the small gardener's cottage behind this property in 1939, and eventually they built a lovely summer home with many fruit trees on the lot. Uncle Béla and Aunt Ili, owners of a beautiful mansion on Gellért Hill in Budapest, decided to rent a large summer apartment in Balatonszemes, immediately next to both Uncle Paul's villa and our own summer residence.

The Csonka grandchildren truly enjoyed the sandy shores of Lake Balaton from 1940 through 1944. While the boys—Paul, John, and Béla—learned to row a boat, the three older girls—Maria, Mazsi, and Melinda—learned how to swim and played in the sand. Meanwhile, the three younger girls—Lívia,

Judy, and Lilla—spent many hours just sitting on one of the many small islands, or in two inches of warm water during the months of July and August, when the water of the lake became very shallow.

A personal tragedy struck my immediate family in July 1943. My grandfather on my maternal side, Károly (Charles) Simon, died of a heart attack at age sixty in Budapest. His wife, my grandmother, Kornélia Simon (age fifty-six), and their unmarried daughter, Lili, were heartbroken, as was my mother, Nelli Simon Csonka.

Károly Simon was a retired principal and mathematics teacher at an elite private Catholic all-girls school in Budapest. In his retirement he was appointed the superintendent of Hungarian Catholic education. He traveled to major cities in Hungary to make sure that the required high educational standards were kept uniformly during final examinations on the national level.

After my grandfather's death, my mother, Aunt Lili, and Grandma Simon decided to wear nothing but black dresses for an entire year to underscore their period of mourning. My brother and I hated these black dresses. Somehow, they symbolized for us the beginning of something dark, gloomy, and dreadful in the political life of the country. Soon enough, our skies were literally black.

In August 1943, American warplanes bombed the railroad hub of Székesfehérvár, directly on the route between Budapest and the Lake Balaton area. This aerial attack was a major hit, disrupting travel and transportation to a huge area. Grandma Simon and Aunt Lili were on the train traveling to Balatonszemes when the railway station was bombed. Their train had pulled out of the station just minutes before the attack (which killed the station master of this busy hub, who was a dear family friend). Hearing the air raid siren, my grandmother and aunt quickly left the train and crawled under it to protect themselves, while the barrage from the machine guns was aimed at the train. The air raid lasted about ten minutes with warplanes crisscrossing the sky above. Finally, the attack was over, and the passengers could climb back into the train, which took them to their destination at Lake Balaton.

My mother and I were waiting for them at the little railroad station of Balatonszemes. Since this attack occurred soon after my grandfather's death, it was easy to recognize my grandma and aunt in their black dresses. To my great dismay, they were literally trembling as they descended the train. For days, they displayed symptoms of shell shock. I can still see my grandmother's long, black and silver earrings bobbing back and forth as her head trembled for days. Finally, the symptoms subsided and they could find peace and comfort in our home.

The next summer at the lake was even more difficult. The adults sat around our supper table discussing the terrible political situation with the Russians approaching from the east and the German army occupying Hungary. They knew that war was inevitable. But what to do about it? The men were very worried about leaving their wives and children at Lake Balaton. Should they leave their families at a place where food was plentiful? Or should they take them home to Budapest so that everybody could be close to the grandmothers and other members of the family?

During August 1944 my family experienced a real shock when we witnessed a terrible confrontation between a small Russian airplane and a Hungarian Stuka plane right above our heads. It happened when my mother and a couple of the children, including me, were enjoying a swim in Lake Balaton. We were in about four feet of water when we heard a great racket above and saw the Russian plane being chased by the Hungarian one. "Everybody, quickly, get down under the water, and stay there as long as you can," yelled my mother. I remember how fast I dove and how long I stayed underwater, holding my breath. When I came up for air, I saw the two planes right above my head. The machine guns peppered the waters right around us. "Kids, go back underwater again," ordered my mother. So, I went down again trying to disappear from the pilot's view. By the time I resurfaced, the two airplanes were gone. We had no idea what had happened. To our knowledge, the chase did not end with the downing of either of the two warplanes. But what a horrendous experience for all of us!

Later that summer, my mother was reading on our patio in the evening when I woke up from a deep sleep because a blinding, terrible light was lighting up the entire sky. "What on earth is this?" I asked her. She said it was a "Stalin candle," actually a tracer rocket that was shot up into the evening sky to help the Hungarian pilots see better when they were fighting it out with the small Russian planes over the lake. It became obvious that the route between Lake Balaton and Budapest, some 138 kilometers away, was becoming a strategically important line for aerial attack between the domestic airplanes and the Russian warplanes. And, in fact, as it turned out, the most important battles of Central Europe were fought over Lake Balaton in 1944.

Yes, the war came closer and closer to our peaceful world of Balatonszemes. In August and September 1944, a series of air raids by Allied forces bomber planes destroyed many Hungarian cities. Two Hungarian oil refineries near Lake Balaton were blown up. After some agonizing discussions, my father, Uncle Paul, and Uncle Béla appeared in their respective cars in Balatonszemes on September 26. They had decided to take us home. The women were told, "You can no longer stay at the lake. We will all leave at the crack of dawn for Budapest."

Mother, Aunt Margó, and Aunt Ilike began frantically packing the essentials for their families. At this very stressful and confusing moment, when my mother was in the process of organizing our medicines, my three-year-old sister ate a whole box of laxatives (she knew they tasted like chocolate). At her wit's end, my mother ran frantically with little Judy to the clinic of our dear trusted doctor, Dr. Ödön Kiss, late at night. "Just give your little daughter three glasses of lukewarm water and nothing will happen tomorrow as you are heading to Budapest," said the doctor. Well, he was right. My mother gave Judy three glasses of warm water, and no "accident" happened on our historic ride back home to Budapest.

And, a historic ride it was! Father, Uncle Paul, and Uncle Béla were driving their respective families home on the two-lane highway from Balatonszemes to Budapest. It was an unforgettable, terrible trip! The highway was dominated by an endless convoy of German trucks and military vehicles, all heading to the capital. We constantly had to ride on the shoulder of the narrow road because the German trucks were literally trying to push us off. And, once off the road, the German truck drivers would not give us the right of way again. The normally five-hour trip of 138 kilometers became a nightmare. We could make no rest stops, and we could not go to the bathroom.

By late afternoon, my totally exhausted father finally decided to leave the highway and take a secondary road on the outskirts of Budapest, in the industrial area of the city. The German trucks were no longer chasing us, but we were terrified by what we saw happening around us. There were burning factories, one after another, with the local fire companies unable to extinguish flames that were leaping into the skies. Finally, around midnight, we arrived in Budapest. Grandma Csonka and Grandma Simon (both of whom then lived in the same apartment house at Orlay Street 9 on Gellért Hill) were patiently waiting up for us. I was half asleep at the dinner table, but I still remember the wonderful taste of the Hungarian stuffed peppers (our favorite dish) that my grandmother Simon had waiting for us. That night, everybody slept like a bear.

Rumblings of War

The three Csonka families faced some difficult times once back in Budapest in the fall of 1944. Uncle Paul's folks and my own family returned to our respective apartments at Horthy Miklós Street 31, while Uncle Béla and family returned to their villa on Gellért Hill. (Only after the war when his villa was bombed and uninhabitable did Uncle Béla move his family back to their original home on the first floor of Grandfather's apartment building.) The political situation in Budapest reached a crisis point. At least twice a week, the residents were awakened at night by the sound of sirens, shrieking, signaling the beginning of an air raid. Allied forces warplanes were bombing the capital and the surrounding suburbs of Budapest.

My parents bought extra-warm robes and felt slippers for my brother, John, who turned nine that fall, and for me, then six years old. These clothes were regularly placed next to our beds, in easy reach if we had to go down to the cellar during the air raids. My mother would quickly put warm overalls on little Judy. When the sirens began we had to leave the apartment fast and in total darkness. No candles or flashlights were allowed. We proceeded to the back of the building, and then we walked down the spiral staircase from the third floor to the cellar. Walking down this spiral staircase in the pitch-dark was extremely difficult. You really had to hang on to the railing in order not to fall.

All the residents of the twenty apartments in my grandfather's building gathered in the cellar, sitting on benches that were placed against the walls. A couple of dim light bulbs, hanging from the ceiling, could hardly light up this dreary place. The adults anxiously awaited the end of the air raid, while the children (myself included) thought it funny to see the residents bundled up in robes and jackets over their pajamas. Once the sirens announced the end of the air raid, the people would move back upstairs to their apartments.

Actually, all of us who were living at Horthy Miklós Street 31 were extremely lucky. Our part of the city did not get a direct hit. Other areas in and around

Budapest did not fare so well. One family, our distant relatives in the Rédly family, lost a little boy and a little girl in the bombing attack in Szentendre, just north of Budapest.

By the middle of November, the nightly aerial attacks became longer and more destructive. Therefore, Uncle Paul and my father decided to move their families into the villa of Uncle Béla and Aunt Ilike on Gellért Hill. This move was very wise. My parents knew that the fallout shelter, built by Uncle Paul at Uncle Béla's house just ten minutes uphill from us, would give us much better protection from bombing attacks than the simple cellar in our apartment house.

Our move to Uncle Béla's villa happened very suddenly and under stressful conditions. We left our respective homes behind, and we only took essentials with us to the new location. Before we knew it, nine children, three sets of parents, two grandmothers, one aunt, and our housemaids were living under one roof. Although each family had a sizable bedroom, we were very crowded around the dining room table(s). The bathrooms were constantly in use.

November 1944 was unseasonably warm. The children explored the huge garden on the hillside with its rose bower, stone sculptures, and fun places to play hide-and-seek. There had been no school for us in Budapest since the beginning of October because of the constant air raid attacks. One sunny November afternoon when all of us were playing outside, we heard a tremendous explosion that shook the air around us. We had no idea what had happened. That evening the Hungarian radio announced that one of the bridges over the Danube River that connected Buda and Pest, the Margaret Bridge, had been blown up.

In their desperate attempt to prevent the Soviet troops from approaching the capital, the Germans wired the bridges across the Danube with explosives so that they could be blown up any minute. In January 1945, massive earth-shaking explosions rocked the air. The historic Chain Bridge, the slender and beautiful Elizabeth Bridge, and the Franz Joseph Bridge were blown up. This was followed by the exploding of the Horthy Miklós Bridge and the Railroad Bridge in the southern section of Budapest. These iconic bridges over the Danube at Budapest, which gave our capital its distinguished look, were now helplessly, pitifully dangling in the rushing waters of the river. It was a terrible sight to see the amputated, truncated bridges, which previously had given so much beauty to the panoramic view of the city.

The residents of Buda were now hopelessly separated from their brothers in Pest. The Germans had staged the explosions without announcing anything to the Hungarian public. In the final analysis, the destruction of the bridges did not prevent the Soviet forces from entering the capital. They used amphibious vehicles and crossed the Danube south of Budapest.

A Child's View of the Holocaust

The year 1944 was heavy with political unrest caused by Hitler's unleashing of the darkest powers of Nazi occupation in Hungary. The pro-Nazi Arrow Cross Party, a brigade of henchmen headed by Ferenc Szálasi, ordered the mass deportation of Hungarian Jews after Regent Miklós Horthy was removed from his post on October 14, 1944, by the Nazi forces in Hungary.

There was tremendous anxiety felt by the general Hungarian population about a series of anti-Jewish measures that required every citizen to establish a family tree, free of Jewish blood. The dreaded ancestry laws declared that anyone who had two grandparents who were Jewish was considered "racially Jewish." My mother and father had to spend considerable energy and time procuring documents from church registries and town hall records to attest to the fact that nobody in our family was of Jewish origin going four generations back. Various aunts and uncles and other family members were likewise required to produce a "clean" ancestry chart. This way my family passed the notorious *Árja Párja* law, which required that even the marriage partner (*párja*) of an Aryan should be of Aryan descent. I sensed great anxiety in my parents' behavior as they studied the family documents spread out all over our dining-room table, but as a six-year-old child I never realized how vitally serious the search for a pure family tree was.

Gyuri Császár Sr., the brother of Aunt Ilike, traveled every Wednesday in the fall of 1944 to Nógrádverőce on the Danube, north of Budapest. He claimed that he bought food for his family. Nobody in our family knew, however, that he also visited the caves near Nógrádverőce, to deliver food to Jews who were hiding there. And, nobody in the family suspected that he was being watched by spies from the Arrow Cross Party. And, of course, nobody anticipated that he would be killed by an Arrow Cross sharpshooter on December 31, 1944, when he looked out the window of his home after a house search by the Nazis. (Uncle Gyuri was the father of Gyuri Császár Jr., about whom you will hear more in the section called "The Parachute.")

Uncle Gyuri was not the only one taking tremendous risk by helping the persecuted Jews of Hungary. Again and again, my father and his brothers showed great heroism in opposing the Nazi forces of Budapest. My father, as the co-owner of the Csonka factory, had established a school of apprentices who were being trained to become mechanics and machine operators for the equipment manufactured in the plant. Fourteen young apprentices in this group were Jewish. During the summer of 1944, many Jewish men on various farms in Hungary were rounded up and deported to forced labor camps. Their wives were allowed to remain at the farms to care for animals and manage the estate. These women, however, were seriously shorthanded and lacked manpower at harvest time. My father realized this and allowed his Jewish apprentices to return home to help their mothers with gathering the harvest. Every morning my father took the punch cards of these fourteen young men in the factory and methodically punched them in, and then he punched them out at the end of the day for several weeks, as the situation demanded.

My father did not realize, however, that he was being watched and that someone had reported his behavior to the German military officer assigned to the plant. Suddenly one day, the German officer burst into his office, locked both doors, and held a revolver to my father's temple. "I will shoot you now, for protecting all your Jews," the officer bellowed at the top of his voice. At this point my father's voice started to tremble, but he said very calmly, "Oh, I am sorry for you…I just see your wife… along with your four children…now that they have killed you!" These few words hit the officer in his heart. He lost his nerve, and slowly said to my father, "Oh, you…go…I will not shoot you." Thus my father, a very brave man, was spared his life.

As co-owners of the Csonka factory, my father and Uncle Béla helped the Jewish organizations in important ways. For example, they secretly donated wagons of food to the organization of the Swedish diplomat, Raoul Wallenberg, which saw that the shipments were delivered in utmost secrecy to the persecuted Jews in several locations of Hungary.

My parents were very cautious not to talk about my father's involvement in protecting the Jews. Yet, in January 1944, my mother shared with us children her anguish about the fate of the persecuted. One evening she declared that from now on we will pray for Jews every night. As a young child, I did not understand why we should pray for the Jews. I responded by saying, "From tonight on, I will pray for the Eskimos and the Indians too." "Why would you want to pray for the Eskimos?" my mother asked. "Well," I said, "because they have such a hard life, surrounded by the sea and the ice at the North Pole." "Well then," she answered, "Maria, you will pray for Jews and Eskimos and Indians every evening." And, so I did.

I did wonder why the situation of the Jews was so different that we should pray for them. Mother did not tell us children about deportations and death camps. In retrospect, I realize she wanted to shelter us from the horror of the historical events that were going on while we were young.

In the spring of 1944, it became public knowledge that Hungary's regent, Miklós Horthy, was secretly negotiating with the United States and Great Britain. Horthy wanted to remove Hungary from the alliance with Germany. To punish Horthy, Hitler decided to occupy Hungary on March 19, 1944. On this fateful day, German military powers overran the country.

Being in Budapest at this terrible time, we found that the climate of the city became unbearable with German military vehicles all around us. My uncles and my father decided to take their families away from the capital before Hitler bombed the city. The brothers packed their respective wives and children into three cars and drove to Mátrafüred, a small resort community in the Mátra mountains, some eighty-five kilometers away from Budapest. This location was far enough from the bombings, yet close enough for the commute by the three working fathers on weekends.

Three sets of parents, nine Csonka children, and three babysitters arrived in Mátrafüred, where we rented a small hotel called Pensió Kovács, managed and owned by a Jewish couple. After spending exactly one night in this pensione, it was obvious the entire building was full of bedbugs. We called in an exterminator, but had to temporarily evacuate our rooms. The next morning the entire family moved to Kékes, a luxury hotel at the highest point in Hungary, in a skiing area. The Kékes hotel was owned by my father's cousin, László Csonka (Laci *bácsi*), a wealthy industrialist.

None of us children had ever been in a luxury hotel before. The boys, Paul, Béla, and John, immediately ran into the bathrooms attached to the hotel rooms and started to fidget around with the bidet, which none of us had seen before. "Hey, this is neat—a fountain in the middle of the bathroom!" they yelled. The jet of water shot up to the ceiling and all of us became soaking wet. Since we had only the clothes on our backs, the three babysitters had to put all of us to bed so our clothes could be laid out to dry overnight, and we children had to have supper in bed. What a delightful adventure!

Spring 1944 in the Mátra mountains turned out to be beautiful. For children like us who never saw a forest before, this should have been a land of total happiness. But a horrible event made our stay in Mátrafüred very difficult. One sunny day in May, our landlords, Mr. and Mrs. Kovács, the Jewish couple, were arrested. I saw them taken away from their hotel by the local gendarmes. The couple had to lock up the room in which they resided and could take nothing with them. They did not say anything to us, the tenants. They were taken away, never to come back again.

This was extremely hard for me to comprehend. I asked my mother to give me a reason why the Kovács had to leave. "Why are the taking them?" I asked. "Nobody knows," was her answer. "Where are they taking them?" I continued asking. "Nobody knows," was my mother's brief reply. While all this was happening, I started to realize how terrible the fate was of people who had to leave family, home, and possessions behind.

During our stay in Mátrafüred, my cousins Paul, Béla, Mazsi, and I had to go to the dentist. My mother took the four of us on the little local train to the county seat of Gyöngyös, some eight kilometers away from our pensione. As we walked toward the dentist's office on one of the avenues in the downtown area of Gyöngyös, which had a large Jewish population, we saw a lot of men wearing a yellow badge, with the Star of David. "What is this?" we children were wondering. "Hush," my mother said, "Don't talk so loud. Everybody in Hungary who is Jewish has to wear this yellow badge." We found this rather unusual, not knowing that this mandate was decreed by the Arrow Cross, the Fascist party of Hungary, following Hitler's orders. We were not totally surprised that our dentist also wore the Star of David. After the dental visit, our little group walked through downtown, and we began counting the men wearing the yellow badge. "How many did you see?" whispered Béla to Paul. And, "How many did you see?" whispered Mazsi to me.

"Oh, stop it, kids," my mother admonished us. "You are not supposed to count. You make a spectacle of yourself."

The early spring in Mátrafüred turned into a very hot summer. More than 43,000 Hungarian Jews were deported to concentration camps that summer. Nothing about this was ever mentioned to us children. The adults did not talk about the news because they wanted to shelter us from these tragic events. In fact, the Csonkas went, as they did every summer, to Lake Balaton, but we did not enjoy the peace and quiet of past summers.

When fall 1944 arrived, my family was back in Budapest following our aborted stay at Lake Balaton. Early in November, one very dark and dreary evening, my mother took me to see a dentist in Pest, on the other side of the Danube. The two of us had to walk home in the dark after the visit rather than take public transportation because the road was blocked with tank-traps—concrete structures that looked like pyramids. As we walked along the Danube banks in Buda, we were terribly downcast. It was obvious that the Russian front was moving very close to us. The Germans were occupying the whole country, but the Soviet forces were digging in, too, encircling the capital, ready for a major attack. There was an eerie silence in the air as we walked. I felt my six-year-old heart sinking in fear of what was going to happen. Suddenly my mother said, "Look, look, down there," as she pointed to the lower banks of the Danube. I saw hundreds and hundreds of people clad in white-and-grey-striped long gowns in a silent procession. "These are Hungarian Jews, who are now marching to the death camps," said my mother. As a young, frightened girl, I finally understood why we had to pray for the Jews.

And, as the horrible year of 1944 was nearing its end, the Fascists of Hungary knew that their rule would soon be over. In a last despicable effort, the members of the Iron Cross Party killed all the remaining Hungarian Jews on the Pest side of the Danube embankment. These henchmen simply threw the bodies of Jews into the water. And the Danube turned red with blood.

Siege of Budapest *(Ostrom)*

March 12, 1938, the day of the Anschluss, was a terrible event in European history. This was the day when Nazi Germany invaded and annexed Austria. From this day on, there was no more peace in Europe.

The outbreak of World War II was a direct and immediate result of this event. It demonstrated that Hitler aimed at territorial expansion.

The Csonkas were fully aware of the danger of Hitler's move into Austrian land. Hungary, as the neighbor immediately east of Austria, felt the tremendous burden of political uncertainty. What if Hitler were to run down Hungary and march toward the Soviet forces to challenge Stalin's power in the east?

Uncle Paul, who spoke English, gathered the family's adults around the radio. BBC radio was very frank about the prospects of an all-out war in which all countries opposing Hitler would lose. I remember with great trepidation the numerous speeches of Hitler, which frightened the general public: "*Wir wollen England ausradieren*" ("We want to erase England") was Hitler's motto. Soon, with the actual outbreak of World War II in Poland, air raids and serial bombings became a reality.

My uncle Paul Csonka Sr. who was a professional architect, was commissioned by the Hungarian regent Miklós Horthy in 1941 to build a state-of-the-art "safe" fallout shelter for him, his staff, and family in Budapest. After completing the construction of the Horthy fallout shelter, Uncle Paul built a similarly "safe" fallout shelter—a bunker—for the Csonka family. Construction began in the spring of 1942 at the villa of Uncle Béla at Somlói Street 6/A, on Gellért Hill in Buda. At this time, my own family and Uncle Paul's family resided at Horthy Miklós Street 31, in my deceased grandfather's apartment house.

Grandfather Csonka's apartment building was certainly not built to withstand an air attack. It was speculated that a bomb (or several bombs) would destroy the building all the way into the cellar, where people seeking sanctuary would be crushed. (And, indeed, in December 1944, this building was hit by a massive bomb attack in which seven residents, including three young children, lost their lives under the collapsed building.) My family and Uncle Paul's family were fortunate that we moved to Uncle Béla's before the bombs fell on our original home.

The bunker, our fallout shelter on Gellért Hill, was purposely not built directly under Uncle Béla's mansion, but to its side. The shelter would remain safe and protected if the building collapsed. There was a series of labyrinthine corridors, with a large number of steps, leading from the mansion into the sub-basement, the basement, and below to the fallout shelter itself. The reason for the labyrinthine corridors was to divert the impact of the tremendous air pressure that would result from the bombs in an air raid attack. At the very foot of the steps leading to the shelter were two double-paneled iron doors with bolts and restraining iron bars on them providing a perfect seal of the doorways with gaskets, if a gas attack should occur. These doors could be closed (somewhat like airplanes' doors) to protect us from intruders' attacks.

After going down the stairs and walking through the double doors, one would finally enter the shelter itself. The shelter was constructed from eight huge, inter-connecting, double-sealed concrete tubes. These tubes were quite large, so that a person of average height could stand up in the middle of the tube. At the far end of the shelter, which was approximately thirty-five feet long, stood an air pump, run by electricity, or if that failed, could be run manually by moving the lever right and left, to pump in fresh air. Immediately to the left of the air pump, at the very end of the shelter, was a small door that led to the emergency exit, to be used if the entrance near the stairway at the other end was inaccessible or had collapsed. The emergency exit led into a long, narrow corridor, lined with bottles of carbonated water for emergency use if our water supply was low or depleted. Unfortunately, during the destructive bomb attack that hit the mansion, all glass bottles exploded because of the tremendous air pressure created by the bomb throughout the shelter.

The emergency exit had a chimney-like construction, with rungs of a ladder built into the wall, leading up to open air. There was a solid concrete roof over the exit that looked like a pyramid, with vents on its four sides for air circulation. The internal construction of the fallout shelter was quite unusual. The walls inside the structure were painted yellow, and two open windows with flower boxes containing geraniums were whimsically painted on the surface of the slightly curving wall.

There were two very long benches that ran along the walls of the shelter for people to sit on, in case we had to stay longer than anticipated. (Nobody, nobody suspected that we would stay for a long nine weeks.) The benches looked like benches on streetcars. They were constructed from long, narrow panels of white maple, and they were screwed down at each end. Behind the curving walls of the tubes there was enough space for storing canned vegetables and fruit. These cans were large and could be seen between the spaces of the wooden panels. (Once, an inquisitive Russian soldier, dressed in a white, quilted cloak noticed the cans. He opened a panel with a screwdriver, took out a can of green peas, punctured it with his screwdriver, and, to our disgust, drank the juice, spilling part of it on the bedding. What a pig!)

While we were still living on the ground and upper levels of Uncle Béla's spacious mansion, our families enjoyed the magnificent view from the hill side of his villa. We could see the Danube with Csepel Island and the surrounding countryside. But at night—to my great horror—we could watch a deadly spectacle from our bedroom windows as the Soviet tracer rockets lit up the sky when they openly attacked the German forces down below in the Danube valley. Bombings and shelling in our neighborhood became more and more frequent. One beautiful old home on the hillside below us was burning with huge flames. My father dragged me to the open window to see it, while I screamed at the shocking sight.

Christmas 1944 was an event that my entire family will never forget. Children and adults sat around three large tables in Uncle Béla's dining room, ready to begin the festive Christmas dinner, with fried fish, potato salad, mayonnaise, chocolate cake, and walnut-poppy seed rolls—the traditional holiday treats. But before we finished our meal, the sirens began to shriek.

This meant: Run to the fallout shelter! I grabbed my new doll, Kati Baba, which I had just received as a Christmas present. We children were told to take our pajamas downstairs, "just in case we have to stay for a longer time." None of us had any idea that we would live underground for the next sixty-three days.

Upstairs, in the mansion, the air was filled with the smell of gunpowder and smoke. All the windows were blown out by the pressure of the air raids. The German troops, our allies, securely nesting in the "citadel" at the top of Gellért Hill above us, were now openly attacked by Soviet forces. The Soviets were using cannonades and bombing attacks to smoke out the Germans.

Uncle Béla's villa on Somlói Street was right in the middle of the battle. Above us were the Germans, and below in the valley the Soviets. It was a scene of total pandemonium for everyone who lived on Gellért Hill. None of us at the Christmas dinner table was aware that at 6 p.m. Christmas Eve the Soviet military commander, Marshall Voroshilov, gave the summary order to begin the direct offensive against the Germans. At this moment, the siege of Budapest began. And from that moment on, the Csonka family of eighteen—nine children, three sets of parents, two grandmothers, and one aunt—plus three kitchen helpers spent nine weeks underground.

On the first morning in the shelter, the electricity went out and our water supply was cut. The family had to resort to burning candles, which we had stored in large numbers in the event that there was no electricity. These candles, used sparingly, gave minimal light. We looked at each other in semi-darkness. Silhouettes rather than real people were all around us. And from what we were hearing, it was obvious that the siege had begun. Grenades were exploding and the constant rat-a-tat-tat of machine guns filled the air. Here and there, large detonations were heard.

My two uncles and my father went upstairs to the mansion and took down several doors. From these doors they constructed beds for the children. During the day, the doors would be flipped up against the wall, and at night, they were turned down so they could be used as beds for us. The older children were safe in these beds, but for the younger ones, the men used string netting that they extended between the ceiling and the bed so that the little ones would not fall out. At night, the adults slept on the floor, covered with big rough heavy charcoal-grey blankets that came from our factory.

Jenny Mama and Aunt Mária were situated close to the entrance of the shelter. They slept in an armchair for nine solid weeks. Next to this area, standing on four legs midway in the air, was an unusual bed that we called the flying carpet or flying box. This was the permanent bed of my cousin Melinda, who was handicapped. We other children were very jealous of this private bed, with its soft blankets and pillows, and we took turns sleeping in it during the daytime.

One level above the fallout shelter was the basement kitchen. We had three helpers, who were heroic in their efforts to stay with us during the siege. My own former babysitter, Rézi, chose to stay although my parents told her she could go home to her family near the Austrian border. Cooking became a real problem for twenty-one people. We had food items, but no water. The shellings and bombings, with their incessant roar came closer and closer to us. Only in the early morning hours, from 2 a.m. to 4 a.m. did the machine guns stop. It was then that Uncle Paul and Rézi ventured down the hillside, with a bucket in each hand, to fetch water from the well in the basement of the Church of the Lazarenes. The whole neighborhood used this well for drinking water, and it saved our lives. But often, as my uncle and Rézi were climbing uphill with their four buckets of water, the machine gunning started up again. They had to lie down on the ground, and, when the shelling let up, run uphill with the water until they were safe inside the house. Very often, there was only a little water left in the buckets by the time they made it back safely. Yet, because we needed the water desperately, Uncle Paul and Rézi risked their lives again and again in their effort to bring us water for drinking and cooking.

After a while, a crisis broke out with the candles. These were thick, long church candles, which were supposed to give us long-lasting light. But to our consternation, we discovered that half of the candle was hollowed out so it could be placed on a special candle holder in a church. Nobody anticipated this. The wick burned for a while and then it collapsed inside the hollowed-out part. What to do? My grandmother and Aunt Mária took these candle remnants, melted them down in the kitchen above us, and re-poured the wax into new candles, using twine as wick. These recycled candles gave out very poor light, but it was still better than having no candle at all. As it turned out, we got very lucky with the candles. At the time the siege ended, we had only a few candles left.

Staying in the fallout shelter for endless time was very boring. At first, our mothers read us stories by candlelight while the children used colored pencils to color pictures in the books they got for Christmas. But after a couple of weeks, people's nerves began to get frazzled. In order to boost morale, my father organized a singing group for the children every morning. While the other adults put away the bedding and raised the beds so that we could once again sit on the long benches, my father began singing with us. "What should we sing today?" he would ask. "Well, let's sing the song, 'Once I and a pretty lover, a lovely brown eyed gypsy girl,' or perhaps the military song 'Captain, captain who sits on his high horse.'" Singing did many good things for all of us, cooped up in a tiny tunnel day after day. We stretched our vocal cords, started to laugh, and generally developed a more positive attitude toward an otherwise dreary day.

Often my father took the older six kids (three boys and three girls) out into the fresh air, immediately behind the mansion. We children were white as ghosts from being underground for such a long time. The cold winter wind turned our cheeks red again. "Watch out, and stay close to the building," warned my father. "There may be a sharpshooter or a soldier with a hand grenade sneaking by behind us." So, we were very careful. Yet, as we were throwing snowballs one day, my brother John (who was always accident-prone) suffered a deep cut next to his nose from a sharp metal object that was inside a snowball. His forehead started to bleed profusely, so my father took him in the car to the nearest first aid station. The whole family became anxious because it seemed like an eternity before the two of them returned. Once safely home, they explained that the car had run into a barrage of gunfire that came from all directions—not an unusual occurrence.

There were troubles with John's health earlier. On December 10, before the siege, he came down with a grave illness, was almost paralyzed, and had to be rushed to Saint John's Hospital, which was far away in another part of Buda. While driving there, he and my father found themselves again in fierce street fighting between German and Russian troops with bullets flying all around them. No sooner had they arrived at the hospital when all the lights went out. John was examined and went through a spinal tap, all by candlelight, with my father holding the candle. Meningitis was the diagnosis. Once the spinal fluid was drained, John started to feel better and his range of movement improved.

In the midst of this emergency, a German military convoy pulled up to the large terrace in front of the mansion. Out came a German officer, who arrogantly declared, "The view from your terrace up here is an ideal spot for our military unit. We will deport you from here so that we can begin setting up our equipment and troops in this perfect location." Mother, a real tigress, jumped up and yelled at the officer in German, "No, no way! No way! Can't you see that we have a very sick boy here, he has a high fever. Can't you take mercy on us? Go away. Don't block our driveway!"

Well, the officer took my mother's combative words in good spirits and did take mercy on us. He made the convoy turn around on our side terrace and began to direct the trucks down the hillside, on the serpentine road. Nevertheless one of the trucks took the wrong turn. As the driver was aiming the truck to the lower entrance of our property on the road below, he hit a tall pink marble column, which was a section of a large archway over the entrance driveway. The column broke into pieces and fell right on the truck. "Good for you," yelled my mother. "Don't block the driveway. Get out of here fast so that my husband can take our sick boy to the hospital."

Getting out of the fallout shelter and into the fresh air in the protected area behind the house—which had been so enjoyable for the children—came to a quick end. One morning in early January, a hand grenade was tossed against our back exit door. The damage was extensive and the door was demolished. No problem. The three Csonka brothers replaced the door with another one. The next morning, this door was ripped apart by still another grenade. No problem. The men replaced this door as well. Needless to say, the next morning, among the shower of grenades that fell around the house, a third door was likewise demolished. At this point, we had a big gaping hole where there had been a door. The brothers left it open on purpose. Instead they took a new door and laid it flat on the ground over some steps leading into the basement. Under the door, they installed a system of bells. Whenever anyone stepped on the door, an alarm bell would sound below in the fallout shelter. This was a very clever and extremely important installation. During the nights, when newly arriving Russian soldiers started to come into our building looking for women, they stepped on the flat door and woke up the men, who were nervously waiting for intruders. The ringing of the bells woke up young and old as well.

During our nine weeks in the fallout shelter, tremendously big bombs were dropped on the property. There were seventeen huge gaping craters in the garden alone. We felt lucky that the house had been spared during that period of time. We children were never told about the dying German soldier that my family took in. If the Soviets had known that we cared for a German soldier, they would have immediately shot someone in my family. Our three maids also nursed a young badly injured Hungarian soldier, and they were deeply saddened when the young man died. The maids buried him in one of the big bomb craters.

The middle of January slowly rolled along. The Soviet front moved closer and closer toward the German troops on top of Gellért Hill, above us. We heard louder and louder skirmishes, bombs, and grenades. Endless machine gunning blasted the air. On January 20, a big red parachute was dropped close to the house. The men in the family planned to remove the parachute from the tree on which it had landed because they thought it was a target for future bombing of the area.

On January 22, my father was in the shelter making a little wooden jewelry box by candlelight. The box was to be a present for my mother, who had her birthday on January 24. Late in the morning, the shelling and the roar of the airplanes became so intense that it was unbearable. We were deathly frightened. It seemed that an airplane was immediately above us. At about 11:30 a.m. the bomb fell on the mansion. It caused such a horrific explosion that the entire fallout shelter shook—it felt as if the interconnecting concrete tubes would wrench apart. The strong wind from the explosion doused the candlelight. We were left in total darkness. The many bottles of carbonated water in the emergency room blew up with a terrible whooshing sound. And then we heard my father's loud cry, "Lord, have mercy on us." This agonized plea made me more scared than the explosion. It made me realize how frightened my own father was.

The explosion brought thick, dark smoke into the shelter. My cousin, young Béla Csonka, ran to the air pump at the back wall of the shelter. He started to operate the pump manually so that we would get fresh air. This was a very heroic act from a seven-year-old boy!

The explosion also burst the water main under the fallout shelter. Below our feet, the hollowed out area of the tubes was filled with water. From that moment on, whatever we dropped on the wooden floor—red pencils, scissors, tape, spoons, glue, etc.—went right through the cracks and landed in the water.

The moment they heard the airplane approaching, all kitchen personnel ran down into the labyrinth corridor leading to the fallout shelter. They all were saved because this passage way protected them from the impact of the tremendous wind created by the explosion.

Little Judy, age three, was sitting on the potty near the entrance of the shelter when the bomb fell. She was knocked over by the impact of the explosion and hit the wall behind her. She sustained a slight cut to her left eyebrow that bled a little. Although this was a minor accident, Judy has a permanent scar, and her eyebrow started to grow in two directions. My sister, now in her seventies, is here to tell her children and eight grandchildren about her unfortunate accident.

Not everybody survived the terrible impact of the explosion. Grandmother Nelly Wotzasik, the mother of Aunt Ilike, was killed by the bomb. She did not leave the kitchen area in the sub-basement when the airplane was approaching. She was a terribly depressed woman, who was grieving the recent death of her son, Gyuri Császár (killed by a sharpshooter on December 31). She was also deeply affected by the death of her five-year-old grandson, Charley Ipolyi, who was killed when the bomb fell at the apartment house at Horthy Miklós Street 31. The forceful impact of the explosion pushed Grandma Nelly, who was lying in a bunk bed facing the wall in the kitchen, into the concrete wall. She was found lying there dead. My father and two uncles had to bury her in the midst of the incessant machine gunning and shooting around them. Only after carrying Grandma Nelly's body out of the house, did the men realize that the entire mansion was burning!

The bomb that hit it was called a phosphorous bomb. It crashed through the roof into the middle of the house, ripping through the living room floor of the mansion and landing in the garage, exploding the three family cars filled with gasoline.

The bomb also tore open the wall of the cellar, where coal was stored for the winter. The fire spread rapidly and ignited the coal. My father, two uncles, and three housekeepers worked incessantly for hours to contain the spreading fire. They used shovels and pitchforks to spread out the glowing coals before they could endanger the adjacent fallout shelter.

There was no fire brigade in the neighborhood, and no water! The only thing that could be used was snow. However, nobody dared to venture outside the house because airplanes were circling above us and machine guns were bombarding us from all directions. The fire—somewhat contained—burned for three days. The nights were the most frightening because the ignited coal glowed throughout the darkness, and our fathers were afraid that these mounds of embers would be seen by the airplane pilots who would shoot at us again.

By January 25, the bitter, unforgettable smell of the burning house permeated the air. My father took me (against my long protestations) to see the smoldering mansion. Through the gaping hole in the cellar wall, I could see the library upstairs. The books were still on the shelves, glowing. The piano was totally dismembered, the strings and coils sticking out in all directions like some giant octopus. Debris was lying all over. I cried and cried and cried. This was a scene that I will not forget until my dying day. Why did my father want me to see all this destruction? I am still not able to comprehend it. I am sure I would not do this to an innocent little daughter of mine.

With a gaping hole on the front of the house, strangers from the outside could have access to our adjacent fallout shelter without us being aware they had entered. This posssibility made the adults very nervous. It was my own mother whose nerves gave out first. She had brought with her to the fallout shelter a little prayer book, which contained a novena to Saint Jude, protector of people in unusually difficult situations. She started to pray a novena, with the nine children around her. It was really touching to see how dedicated all of us were, kneeling beside her each day for the nine days of prayers.

Day one, day two, day three, and finally a week had passed. We were praying and waiting for a "miracle" to happen. If you really believed in St. Jude (whose name was St. Jude Thaddeus), you were promised that by day nine your prayers would be answered. And, the miracle happened. On day nine, all fighting was over. The Germans were conquered. The Soviets arrived. What a great relief this was! Little did we realize, in our joy, that the arrival of the Russians was not good for us at all. As a matter of fact, the Soviet occupation was just as bad, or worse, than the German occupation. The Russian soldiers looted, raped, and killed. They were veritable monsters. This was some miracle that Mother and the nine of us children had prayed for!

My mother made a solemn oath to St. Jude Thaddeus. She declared if we were saved from danger, if we survived it all, she would name her next-born son Thaddeus in gratitude. And, indeed, after the war was over, a boy was born to her whom she named László Miklós Tádé (Tádé being Thaddeus in Hungarian).

The Russians Are Coming

The victorious Red Army arrived in Hungary in early spring 1945. At first, there was unimaginable relief when the Germans were defeated and the shooting stopped. But the relief turned into indescribable terror when my family found out that bands of drunken Russian soldiers were roaming in groups, going from house to house in our neighborhood to rape women. Soon they were raping and killing women wherever they went. The women were the "spoils of war."

When my father and uncles heard the disturbing news circulating about the roaming bands of drunken Russians, they were very worried about the women in our fallout shelter. They developed a plan for hiding our women in a huge, unoccupied room in the sub-basement of Uncle Béla's home, which had been set up with beds and bedding for temporary emergency use. Every evening, my mother, Aunt Margó, and Aunt Ilike disappeared into this room. The only women who stayed with the men and the children were Grandmother Csonka and Aunt Mária, her forty-three-year-old unmarried daughter. They were not afraid of the Russians, and they willingly risked their lives in order to protect the children.

Every afternoon, my father and uncles escorted four additional women—two cousins and two aunts—to Gellért Hill for safety in the sub-basement room with the beds. Our three housemaids also spent the night in that special room. Once everyone was accounted for, the men covered the entrance with a giant piece of brown paper. In front of the brown paper, they placed a tall and wide bookcase filled with children's toys and kitchen utensils. This way, the huge door was perfectly concealed. The women behind the door were in darkness, with only two candles to light the huge space. The women were told to whisper just in case a Russian soldier was prowling nearby. We, the children in the fallout shelter, were also in the dark, not suspecting anything, although I vaguely remember missing my mother. I was wondering, "Where did all the women go?"

Then, in the middle of one night, the bell began to ring. That meant that someone stepped on the door upstairs as they crossed into the side entrance of the house. When the bell began ringing, Uncle Paul banged on an empty bucket, long and hard, with a hammer. This was the signal for the women in the special room to: "Shut up, the Russians are coming."

And, the Russians came. They brought large flashlights and began searching the entire fallout shelter. They were obviously looking for something. The Russian soldiers wore heavy, white quilted coats, which would not be noticed in the snowy landscape of their homeland. On their heads they wore furry "Russian" caps with the red, five-pointed star in the middle. Each of these men seemed to be extraordinarily huge. One soldier came directly up to me as I was lying in my bed and took my white fuzzy dog away from me. I began to cry. Then, he gave me chocolate and, finally, gave my dog back. I was thoroughly frightened.

There was an eerie silence in the fallout shelter. All nerves were tense. Our men did not dare to do anything unexpected to the Russians, who were carrying machine guns as they entered. They also had hand grenades dangling from their belts. Finally, the soldiers turned around and left. Total darkness enveloped us again. There was a great sigh of relief from everybody when they were gone. We were especially grateful the Russians had not harmed my grandmother or aunt.

Day after day, the men escorted the women into the secret room at nightfall. Day after day, the men put up the big case with the children's toys in front of the door. But somehow, these terror-filled days passed. There were fewer and fewer Russians entering our shelter at night to look for women, although a good number of Russians were roaming freely in the burned-out house during daytime hours.

Somehow, the brutally cold winter of 1944–45 eased to an end. By the middle of February 1945, all of us dared to venture out of the fallout shelter for longer periods of time to enjoy the fresh air. The huge bomb craters everywhere had destroyed the garden. It was an indescribably sad feeling to see the burned-out house on the hill above us. I wandered through my previous bedroom and found the floor filled with plaster and debris. In the rubble, I found my little china bear with its cute face and bow tie. The bear was originally engine red and the bow tie was blue, but now, after the fire, it was a pale white china bear. The two little arms and legs were missing, but I found them in the rubble. I was really happy with my lost-and-found toy! My father put a wire through holes in the arms and legs, and soon I had a perfect bear again. I colored it red with crayons, but the red always faded away.

The Russian military authorities ordered the soldiers to stop raping and harassing women. Instead, the soldiers were permitted only to loot homes. Bands of armed soldiers entered many apartments in Budapest while the occupants were still in fallout shelters. The Russians soldiers literally set out to wreck the homes. They took the contents out of every drawer, put everything in a big pile in the middle of the living room, and then the soldiers urinated and defecated on the pile. And to think that we, the Hungarians, were happy that the Russians had arrived! Surely my mother and we nine children did not pray for such a "miracle."

One day when my father and Uncle Paul were away from the shelter, they were captured by roaming Russian soldiers for *malenkaya rabota*, "a little work." They ordered my uncle and father, plus two other men, to carry a large kitchen stove (which the Russians stole from some home) down a long flight of stairs, and farther down into the valley. My uncle suggested, "Let's just drop this stove on the ground, so that it will break." So, a couple times, as they took the stove down the steps, they dropped it with such force that the stove eventually fell apart, long before they got it to the valley. When the Russians saw what happened, they let the four men go.

Food was very scarce during the siege of Budapest. People were on the brink of starvation. For nine weeks it seemed the Csonkas would eat nothing but dried peas, beans, and lentils. Nobody could even dream about meat. But really? Frozen carcasses of the German soldiers' horses were lying on the side of the roads everywhere. Ordinary people were desperately hungry, so they carved large chunks of the frozen horsemeat and made a stew from it. We ate it, too! Horsemeat, I remember, had a kind of sweet taste to it. It was 100 percent better than eating legumes all the time.

In early spring 1945, the warmth of the March sun invited the residents of Buda and Pest out of the fallout shelters. Life began again.

My father walked back to the factory on Fehérvári Street with Uncle Béla to survey the destruction and to begin again the operation of the workshops. The factory, now under Russian supervision, became the motor for the rebuilding of Budapest. (Wouldn't Grandfather Csonka have been amazed?) Cars, trailers, and tractors were ordered by the Russian military. Soon, the factory began to operate with full force.

Toward the end of March, my father and Uncle Béla found two rooms in the factory where their families could live temporarily until our apartments in Grandfather's building were made habitable again. Uncle Paul, Grandma Csonka, and Aunt Mária returned to the homes where they lived before the war.

April 4, 1945, was the official date for the end of the German occupation in Hungary. From April 4 on, life in Budapest became somewhat normal again. The war was over, but the aftermath lingered. I will never forget the day when my family walked on Fehérvári Street from our factory toward the home of my two grandmothers on Gellért Hill. On the right side of Fehérvári Street was a building, formerly my mother's high school and now a military hospital. In front of the former school was a set of sixteen tennis courts (on which I later learned to play tennis). But that day, these tennis courts had been dug up, and were being used as mass graves. Truckloads of dead, naked prisoners were thrown into the deep ditches, right in front of our eyes. All of these men, we were told, had died from typhoid fever. This was a horrible, horrible sight for an innocent seven-year-old girl to see. The vision of these naked men haunted me for the rest of my life. Mother admonished us as we walked near the open mass graves, "Turn your heads away! Don't look, don't look!" But, in spite of this warning, I looked anyway. I was terrified and yet mesmerized by the sight.

My little sister Judy remembers still another post-war episode. At a certain meadow next to our parish church was a makeshift cemetery for all the infants who were killed during the siege of Budapest. Little graves of babies covered the entire hillside. Judy maintains that she has never forgotten this sad sight and had nightmares about it.

Easter came early in April 1945. My family was invited for Easter brunch with both grandmothers, who now lived in the same apartment on Orlay Street 9. After the brunch, my mother, my brother and sister, and I were walking home toward the factory. As we approached the railway underpass, we heard a terrible, thundering noise from the air. We saw a Russian airplane chasing a German Stuka dive bomber right above our heads. The sound of the machine guns so close scared us all. Shots were falling around us. "Get down on the ground, all of you," my mother yelled. And as the three of us children got down on the pavement, my mother crawled on top of us, protecting us with her body and outstretched arms. All of us were trembling. Later we learned that the Russian plane shot down the German pilot. We were safe, but the peaceful feeling of a warm Easter Sunday afternoon had evaporated.

Life in the factory started to seem normal. We had warm food from the kitchen and bunk beds to sleep in. One day we even had a large tub of warm water, which was brought into the room so that each of us children—not one of us having been bathed for nine weeks—could be scrubbed down with soap and water. My nine-year-old brother cried out in indignation, "Mother, why do you always have to give me a bath?" All of us laughed at John's emotional outburst.

But we were also smiling at the particular question of my little cousin, Lilla, age three and a half, "Mother, how are we going to die, now that the bombs are no longer falling?" As it can be seen from these family anecdotes, humor and normality gradually came back into the life of the Csonka family.

The Parachute

It was May 1945. I was trying on a white, madeira-lace dress, sewn by my maternal grandmother Simon for the big occasion. I, as the seven-year-old daughter of the Csonka factory co-owner, was to greet the Russian military leader, Captain Kolyesnikov, on the stage of the factory. Kolyesnikov was being celebrated in a banquet because he was the newly appointed military director, supervising civilian operations in the Csonka machine factory. Not only was I to greet Kolyesnikov from the stage, I was also supposed to curtsy, hand him a bouquet of red roses, and say these few Russian words: *Zdrastvuyet, gospodin kapitan.* (Hello, gracious captain, sir.)

My family rehearsed these words with me before the big event, but nobody knew that these words would never be spoken by me. Nobody knew that I would never wear the white lace dress. Instead, catastrophic events on the day the banquet was to be held, May 16, totally erased the banquet from our minds forever. At the time we were still living in the factory, but early that day my family wanted to go to Uncle Béla's once-beautiful mansion on Gellért Hill in Buda, some three kilometers away. I walked up the steep stone staircase alongside my babysitter, Rézi, and I clearly remember feeling that I did not want to go. I had some ominous, unexplainable, creepy premonition.

In addition to Rézi and me, the entourage included my siblings John and Judy, and my parents; Uncle Béla and his sister-in-law, Manci Császár; and the Császár sons, George Jr. (Gyuri), age nine, and Frankie, age three and one-half. It was Aunt Manci's husband Gyuri who had been killed by a sniper bullet. Why did all these adults want to go to the abandoned, burned-out mansion, with its living room caved in, and with a huge, gaping hole where the three-car garage had been? Well, they wanted to dig out from the rubble the potatoes, which were still stored in the garage.

While the grown-ups were digging potatoes, the children were unsupervised. We—John, Judy, Gyuri, little Frankie, and me—first roamed around and then we went up on the hillside, directly toward the huge rubble pile that surrounded the emergency exit of the fallout shelter. We were led by Gyuri, always the "team leader in mischief," up the rubble hill, all the way to the red parachute, which we gingerly touched by hand.

Gyuri, at nine, had lots of emotional issues connected to the war, primarily the death of his father. Every day Gyuri came home from the playground with his pockets filled with ammunition, which he picked up from here, there, and everywhere as all the streets and squares of Budapest were littered by bullets left from the heavy fighting. Aunt Manci, who grieved the loss of her husband, had major worries about her son, whom she labeled a "pyromaniac" after she found bullets and military hardware in Gyuri's room. Yet, he was just one of the many young boys who took great pleasure in collecting—and diffusing—the explosives that they found on the ground and in burned-out buildings.

Now, back to the parachute. Gyuri climbed up the walnut tree to the parachute and yelled to us below, "Look, what I found! A whole barrel of explosives!" And yes, we all ran up the rubble hill to look into the barrel. Through the opened side door of the barrel we saw three rows of bullets, lined up in a semi-circular fashion, following the inside curvature of the barrel. "Oh, I take this one!" yelled Gyuri, and we, as sheep, followed him, running down from the heap of rubble to the side of the house. We came to a fairly narrow walkway, with a small strip of grass on it, finished off by a heavy concrete retaining wall, about three feet tall and one foot thick.

This seemed a good spot to find out whether the explosives still worked. So Gyuri threw the bullet against the wall and it started to smoke. At this point, I stepped back because I sensed trouble (and perhaps these few steps saved my life). Gyuri picked up the smoking bullet and threw it against the concrete wall again. It went off with a most horrendous, dull explosion that shook the air in the whole neighborhood. Little Frankie was instantly killed. I was standing to the left of Frankie, and I was knocked to the ground, unconscious. They tell me that my dress was torn in the front, and that blood was gushing out from my left chest area. Gyuri also fell to the ground. He sustained intestinal injuries and got shrapnel in his legs. John, who saw what was going to happen, quickly pulled Judy behind the corner of the house. He himself received some minor wounds from shrapnel in his right shoulder. The adults, who sped toward us when they heard the explosion, were horrified to see three children lying in pools of blood. Our babysitter ran down the hill to the neighboring Russian military police to ask for a doctor and a truck to take us to the only functioning hospital, which was across the Danube in Pest, at Üllői Street. My mother, father, and Aunt Manci accompanied us. The attending Russian doctor numbed Gyuri and me with shots of Novocain. Once in the hospital (named after the famous surgeon

Louis Bakay), I was put under for a major operation. It turned out that I had a deep wound in my left chest cavity such that the escaped air from my lung gave me a condition called "air lung." Today, lung specialists call it pneumothorax. My heart was pushed into the middle of my chest, and I had a number of pieces of shrapnel in my chest. I do not remember the operation itself, only the unbearable pain when the surgeon tried to suction the air out from my chest. "Air lung" in the 1940s was usually a fatal injury. My parents were told that thirty-two soldiers with such injuries had been brought to the hospital, and they all died. My parents were advised that, "Maria will be an angel by tomorrow morning."

I had a horrible night, tossing and turning, constantly kicking my mother, who tried to sleep at the foot of my bed. She believed that I only had a couple of hours to live. But, next morning I woke up and found seven doctors at my bedside. "She made it," they exclaimed, rejoicing. "Yes, because she is so young, she survived this most impossible injury!" Everybody was happy, and I opened my eyes. "Watch out!" yelled one physician. "She has a left eye injury." Really? Nobody realized that I also had an eye injury because I never opened my eyes on the operating table. Now, it was time for eye surgery. This I clearly remember. I hated the doctor who sutured my left cornea because a part of it was torn by shrapnel.

The day after the eye surgery, the doctors brought a huge electromagnet to my bedside. They wanted to see if I had any metal still in my eye. But nothing happened. The magnet did not react, so the eye doctor concluded that there was nothing remaining in my eye. Boy, was he wrong! Only years later, in 1973, when I was living in the United States and had to have my left eye enucleated because of injury-induced glaucoma, did the ophthalmologist fall into shock. It turned out that there was a large piece of metal in my eye, very close to an area that was part of my brain. If the shrapnel had moved, I could have ended up with permanent brain damage, or possible death. The ophthalmologist sent the enucleated eye to Walter Reed Army Medical Center in Washington, D.C. The result of the hospital finding established that there was a piece of copper in the eye. Having such a weak magnetic field, it was no wonder that this piece of copper shrapnel did not respond to the electromagnet back in 1945. By the grace of God, I was lucky to be alive.

My lung injury slowly healed. Finally, at the end of June 1945, I was released from the Budapest Clinic.

The doctors wrote a report in Latin about the fact that I had metal pieces in my chest cavity. With today's medical knowledge, it is surmised that these metal pieces are also made of copper. Thus, I am told that I should never have the technique called magnetic resonance imaging (MRI) because of the danger of electromagnetic reaction of the shrapnel.

What happened to my vision, you might ask. Immediately after the injury, I could read the headlines of the newspaper if it was held up to me. But my cornea developed a grey cataract, which made vision less and less possible. Soon I could only tell light from dark, and by September 1945, I lost all vision in my left eye. What a terrible, life-determining loss!

Because of my May 1945 injuries, I never went to first grade. (That year, due to the war, first grade was compressed into the months of June, July, and August.) Thus, I took a private exam in August so that, with my age group, I could enter second grade in the fall of 1945. As I entered second grade, I had to wear dark glasses to protect my eye. This was a big problem as the boys in the hall ganged up on me and tried to knock off my sunglasses. When four of the boys jumped on me, someone ran to find my brother, saying, "John, come fast, they are beating up your sister!" Well, by the time John arrived, I had successfully kicked and punched all of them, and they gave up bullying me. But I never forgot who they were, and one day in fourth grade, I tripped all four of them on the ice of our school skating rink!

What happened to Gyuri, you may ask. His father and paternal grandmother (Grandma Nelly) were dead, casualties of the war; his little brother Frankie was also dead, killed by Gyuri's own rash actions. Was it fair to call him a murderer, as some family members were prone to do? He had to live life with this burden, plus the knowledge that he had caused me tremendous physical discomfort, injured me for life, and was responsible for the four major eye operations that followed. Gyuri was taken away from his mother's home and placed into a boarding school in September 1945. He was a student of the Benedictine monks on a hillside retreat in Pannonhalma in western Hungary. He would not see his family for three years. Yet, he matured, grew up, and became a changed person. Once reunited, he appreciated being with family and was seen helping with domestic chores, even ironing the family laundry. When he was older, he became a respected mechanical engineer in my father's factory. He later married and had a family of his own.

Gyuri and I remained "partners in crime" for life. Although at first I could not forgive him, I soon realized that we were both victims of an accident. In the final analysis, he was not the ultimate cause of my injuries; the ultimate cause was the war. I have kept in touch with Gyuri for over fifty years. When in 1980 I went back to Budapest for the first time, Gyuri took me to the hospital where the two of us were treated as patients. Then we drove to Uncle Béla's villa on Gellért Hill. We walked to the very site of the explosion and noticed, to our surprise, that the exploding bullet bit a large piece of concrete out of the retaining wall. A lasting testament to a tragic day.

Having survived such a life-threatening accident made me a changed person. I look at life (and death) from the perspective of a humble individual who is thankful, ever, for the gift of life. I am grateful to God for the medical miracles that made me a fully functioning, healthy human being again. Yes, I had to face and overcome some terrible obstacles in my early years. This knowledge makes me a joyous being, one who is able to see the silver lining in every cloud.

Kornélia Pintér Simon

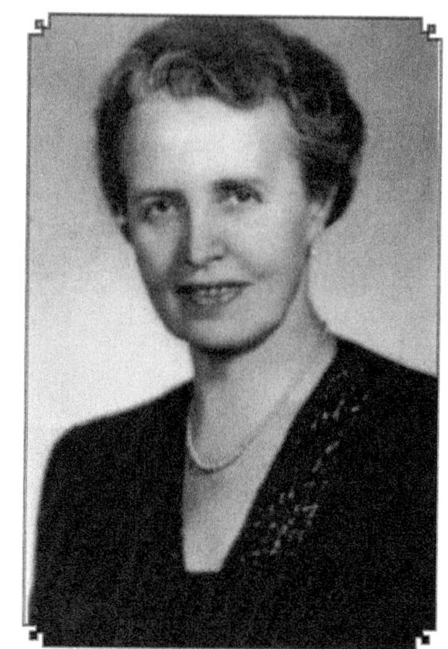

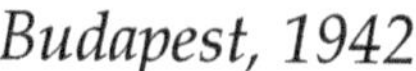

Budapest, 1942

Károly Simon

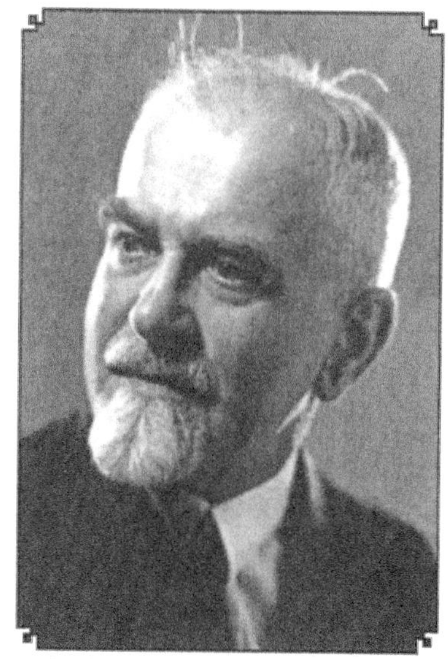

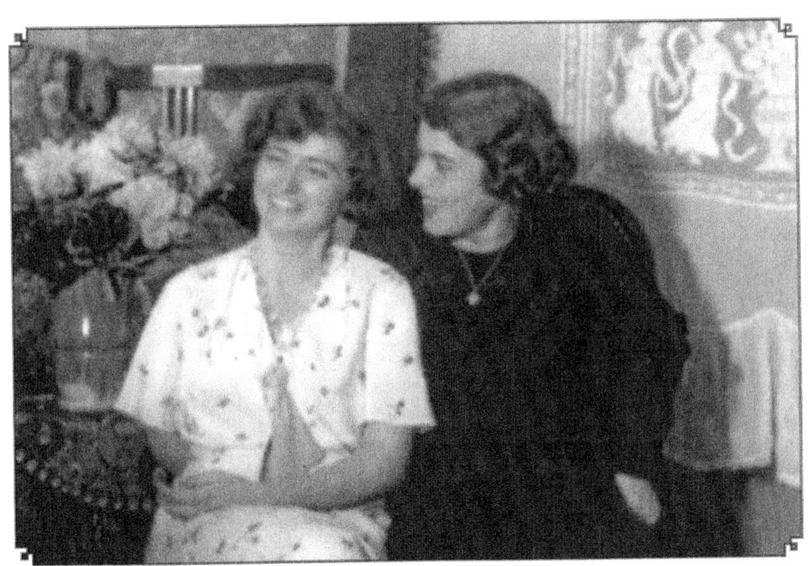

Nelli Simon, on right, on the occasion of her engagement to John Csonka. To the left is schoolmate and future sister-in-law Margó Warga Csonka. 1934

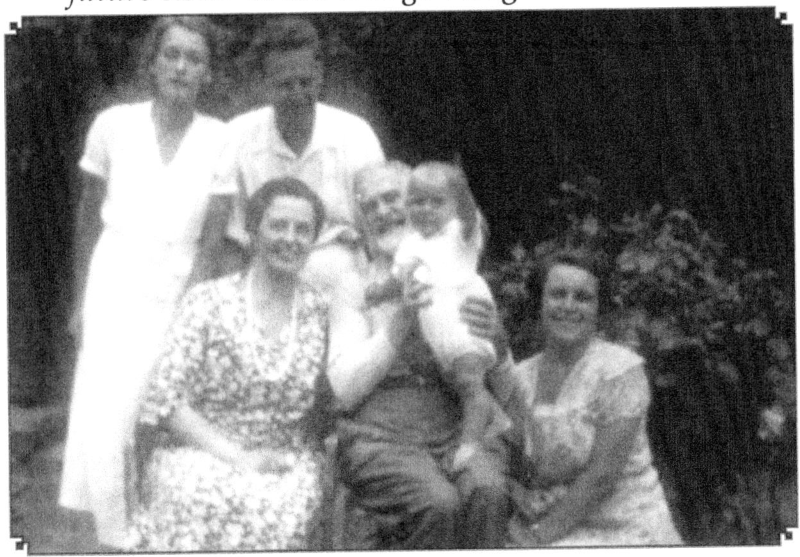

Simon grandparents, seated, with first grandchild, John Csonka Jr. In the rear, Lili Simon and John Csonka. On the right, Nelli Simon Csonka. 1936

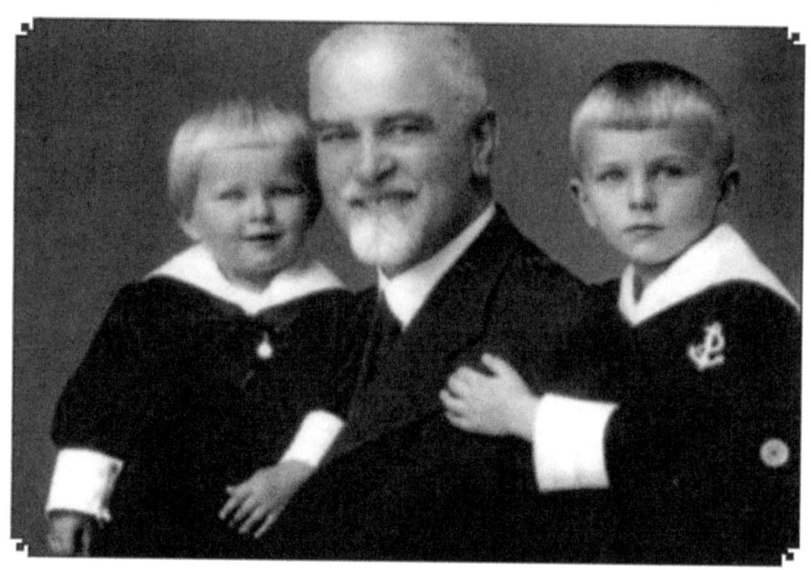

Grandfather Simon with Maria and John. 1940

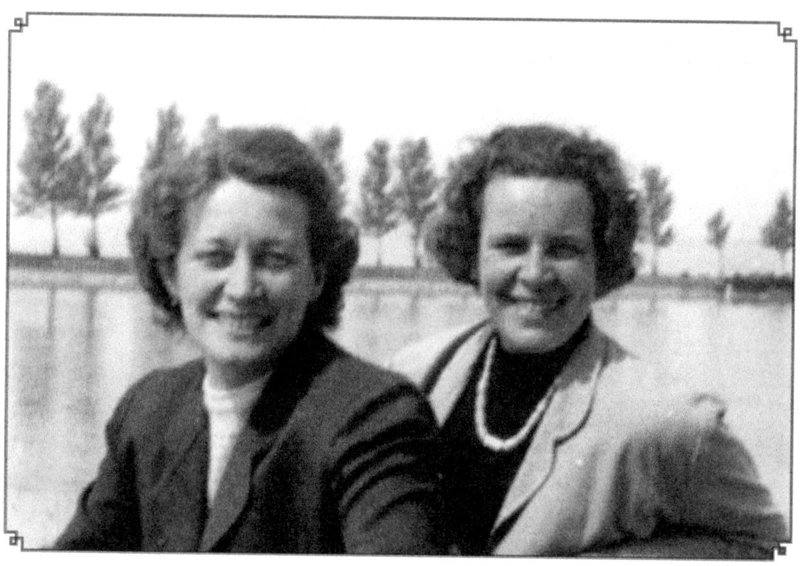

Sisters Lili Simon Vidóczy and Nelli Simon Csonka.
Balatonszemes, 1958

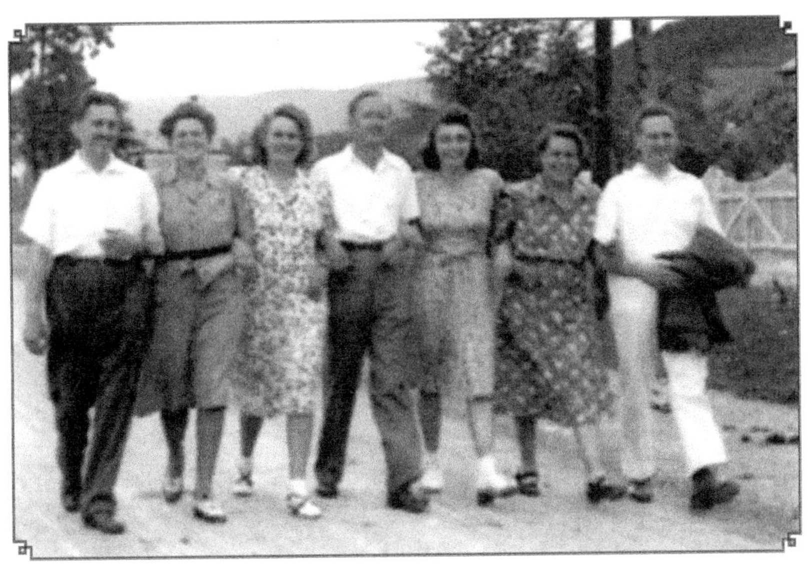

Summer stroll. From left: Uncle Béla and Aunt Ilike; Manci and Gyuri Császár; Manci's sister; my mother and father, Tihany. Lake Balaton, 1942

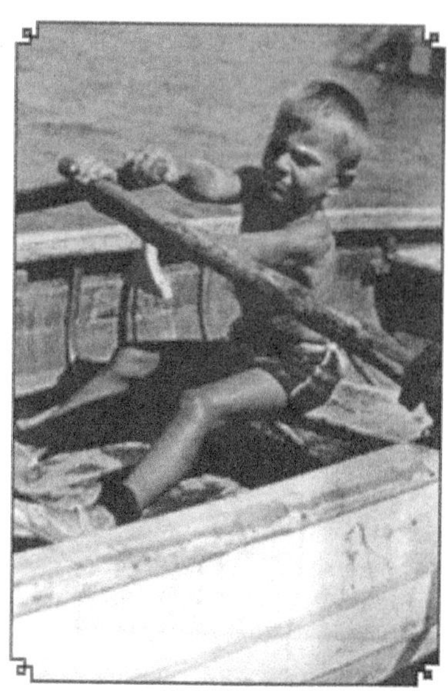

Summers at Balatonszemes.
John, Maria, Judy.
Lake Balaton, 1942–43

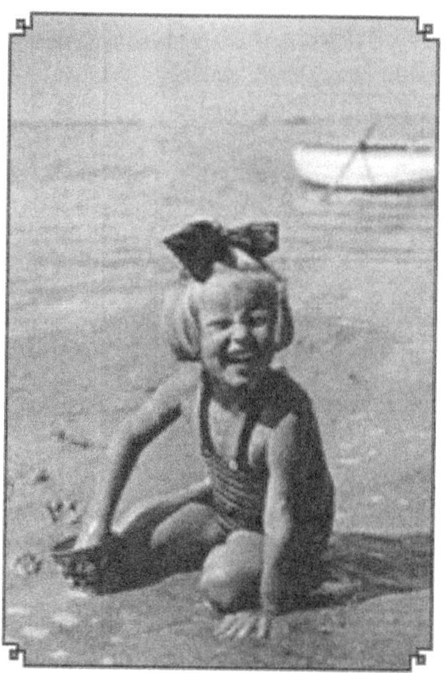

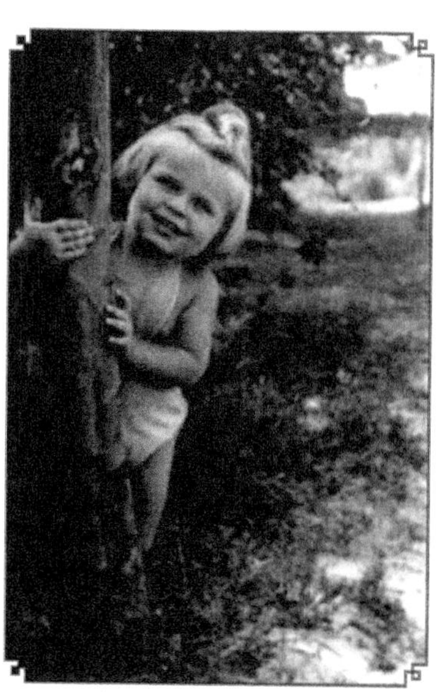

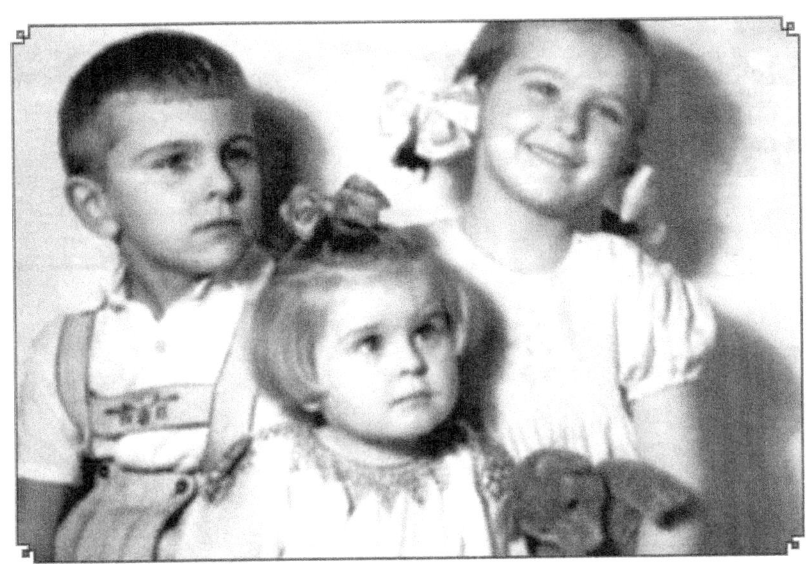

John, Judy, Maria. 1943

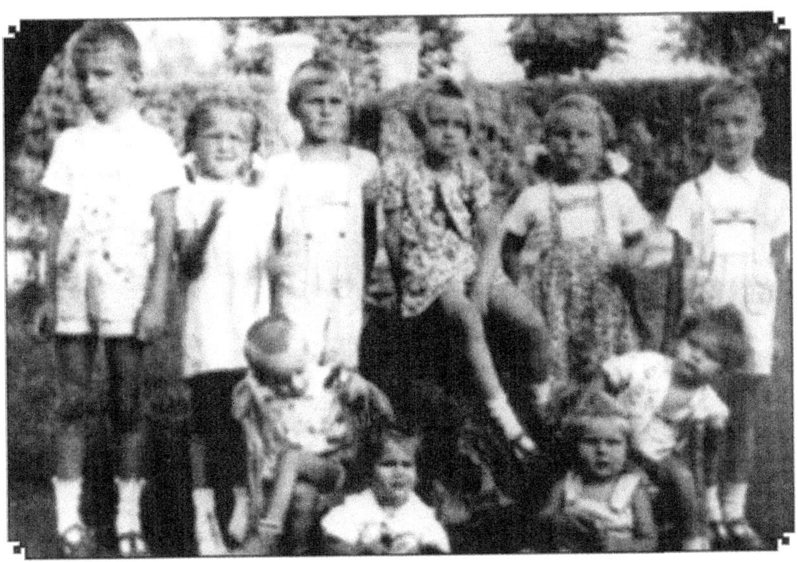

Csonka grandchildren in villa garden in Balatonszemes. From left, standing: Paul, Melinda, John, Mazsi, Maria, Béla; below: guest in chair, Lilla, Judy, Lívia. c. 1943

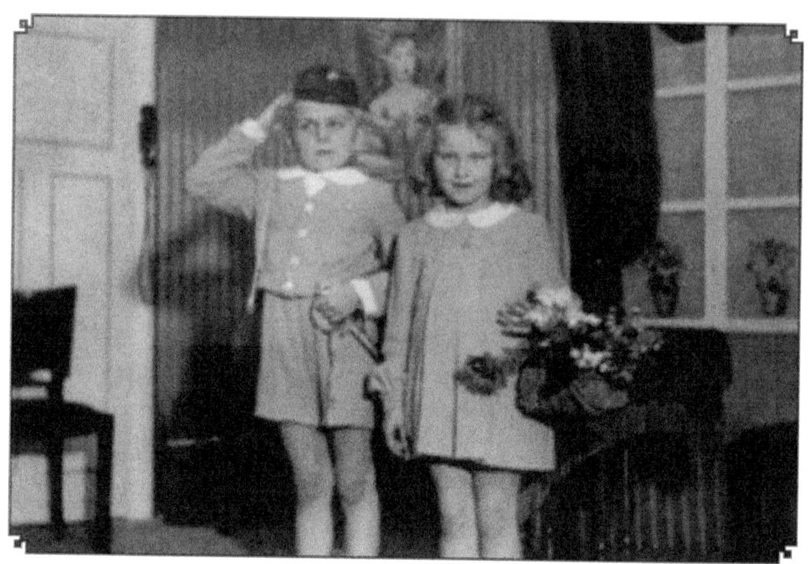

John and Maria on stage at the Csonka factory. 1943

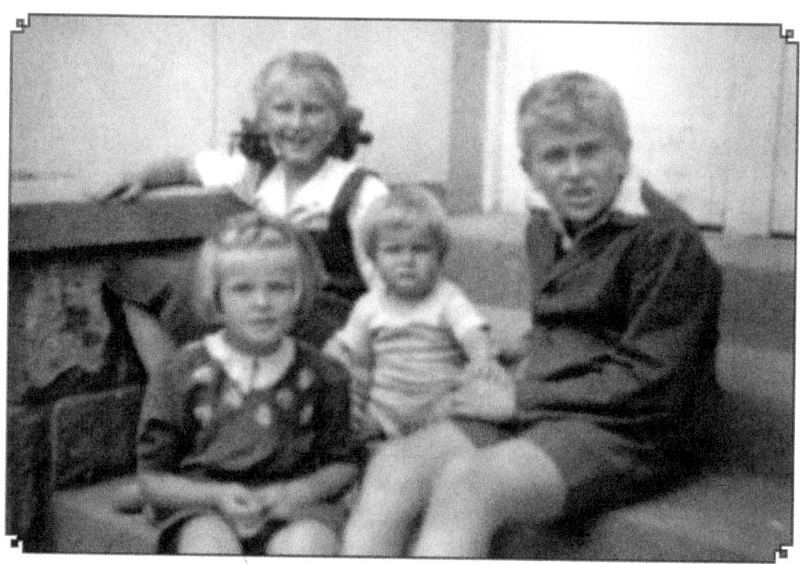

The author and her siblings: Judy, Laci, and John at their villa, Balatonszemes. 1948

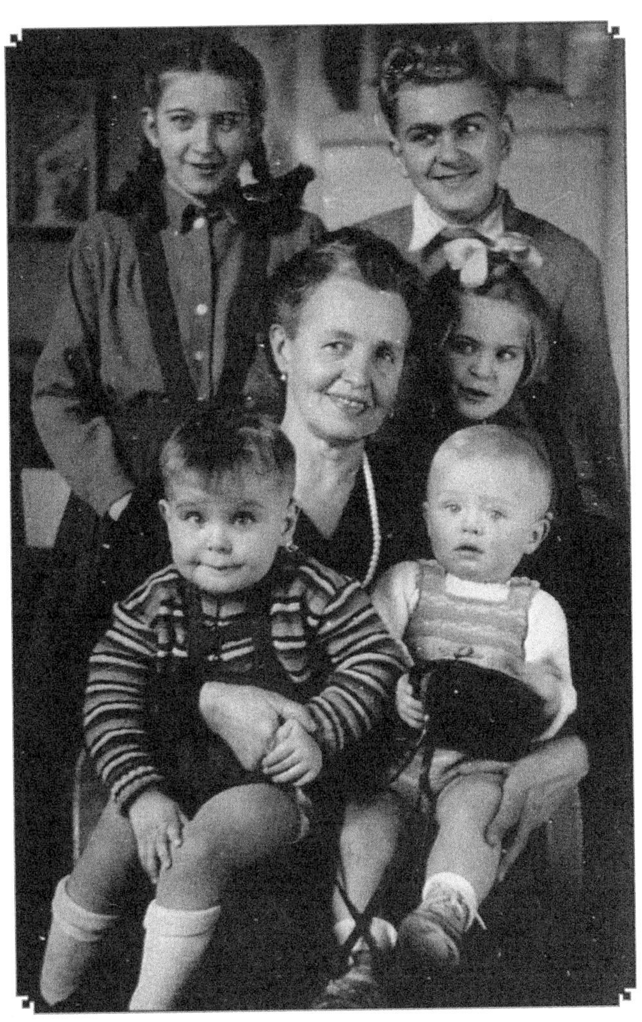

Grandmother Simon with grandchildren Maria, John, Judy, and Laci Csonka, and Tamás Vidóczy. 1949

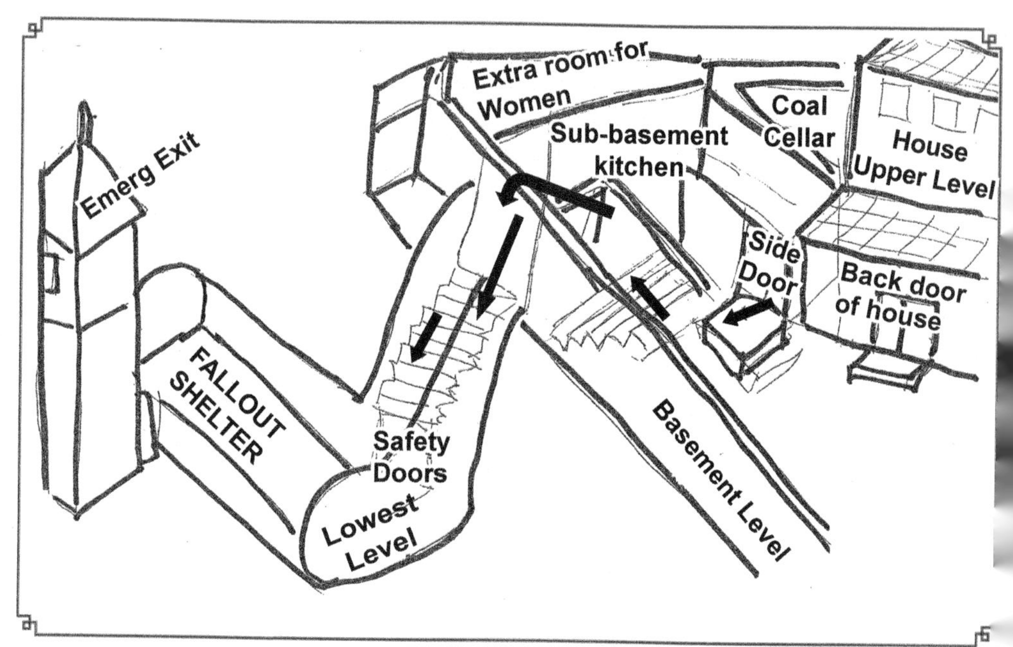

The fallout shelter on Gellért Hill served as home for twenty-one people for nine weeks. The diagram shows the shelter's relationship to Uncle Bela's mansion.

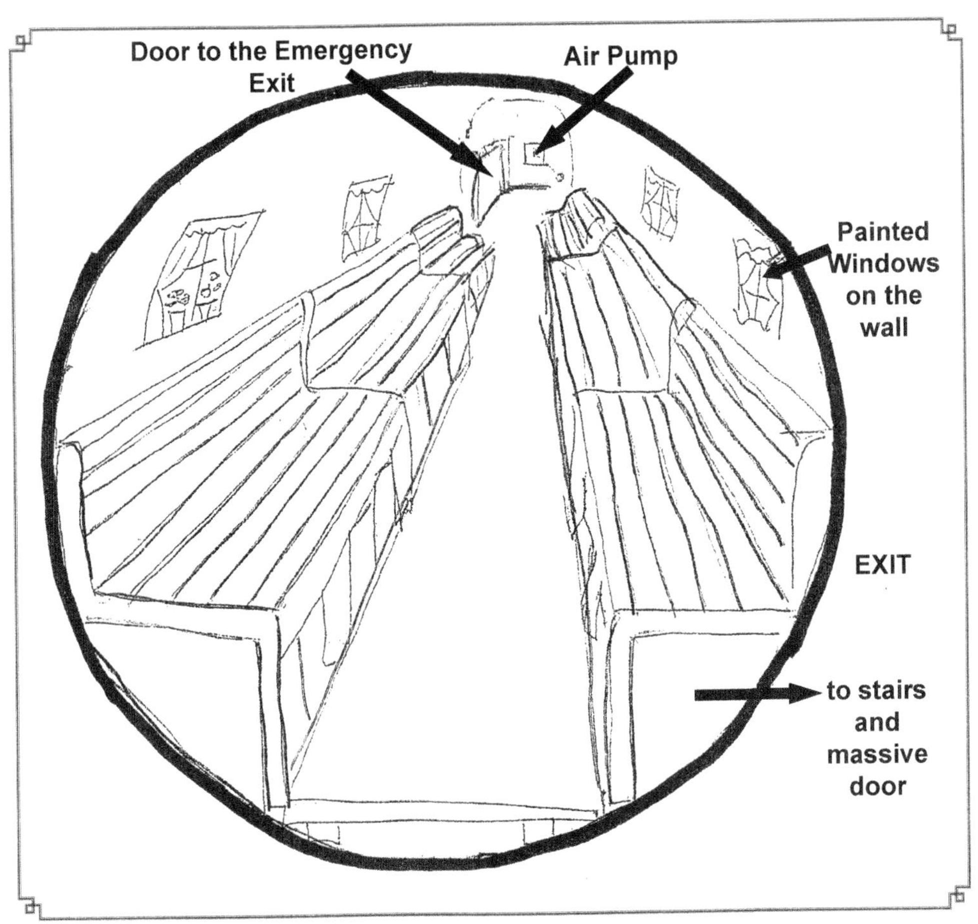

Interior view of fallout shelter depicted during daytime with benches along the two walls. At night, the benches were converted to beds. Pictures of windows with potted geraniums were painted on the sunny yellow walls to create the illusion of not being underground.

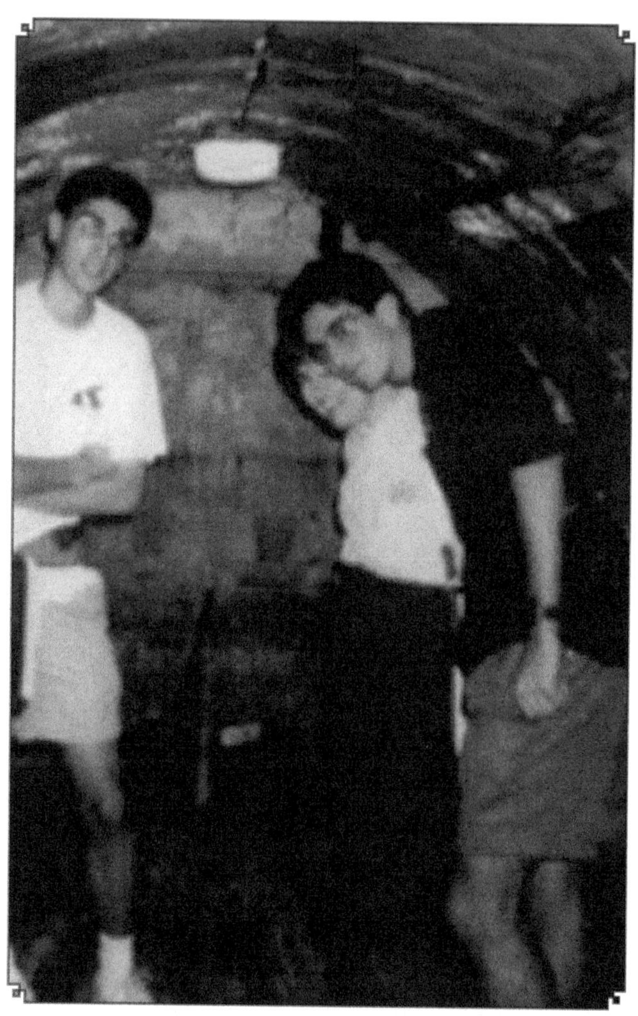

Cousin Lilla, who was three when she lived in the shelter, shows sons Peter and Tony the water marks and decay. Behind them, the handle of the water pump and the faded windows with geraniums. 2001

PART III

The Transitional Years
(1945-1951)

Béla Bartók Street

By June 1945, the John Csonka family was able to move from the factory back into our beautiful, sunny apartment on Béla Bartók Street 31 (formerly Horthy Miklós Street). The Béla Csonka family had to abandon their burned-out mansion on Gellért Hill. They joined us in my grandfather's apartment house, on the first floor. Life began to be peaceful and interesting again.

The apartment house that János Csonka bought during the war years (1914–18) was the scene of many happy events and some less-happy dramas, all of which constitute the memories of my childhood and youth. The name of the street changed, but, with one exception—the new fourth room—the individual apartments remained true to their original purposes. I want to describe our living arrangements, which, I believe, will sound unique in the twenty-first century to those of you reading this who live in unattached houses on private lots. To describe my living arrangements as communal hardly describes the interaction I had with my grandmothers, aunts, uncles, and cousins.

The building was three stories, plus a basement, with twenty apartments. Various relatives lived in various apartments over the years. The three Csonka brothers lived on three different floors in spacious apartments with identical floor plans. Basically, there was a drawing room, a dining room, and a bedroom. Of course, there was also a kitchen, a bathroom, and a maid's room. And from the balcony off the kitchen we had a beautiful view of the trees on Gellért Hill. In our drawing room you would find a round coffee table with four arm chairs and a couch; my father's desk at an angle in one corner; and a sofa in the other corner. The dining room, in addition to a dining table and chairs, had a curio cabinet, a china cabinet, and a baby grand piano in the corner. The bedroom held a double bed, three twin-size beds, and a wardrobe.

Then came the bomb during the war that destroyed the immediately neighboring apartments on all three floors. As part owners of the building, the Csonka brothers paid for the repairs, which took three years. As there were new babies in two of the families, the decision was made to take a room away from the damaged adjacent apartments on all three floors. This, then, became our "fourth room." It came in handy as the family grew and when income was needed. In my family, Judy and I slept in the fourth room on an open-up couch at night, and we had space there for our desks. John slept on the sofa in the drawing room. My parents slept in the bedroom with little Laci in a baby bed next to them.

However, when my father left in 1948, we needed to relocate everyone. The fourth room had a side entrance and a small toilet so that it was easily rented out to university students from 1948 until our deportation in 1951. Judy and I moved back into the bedroom with Laci and Mother. John stayed on the sofa.

After the War

Our first Christmas after the war was a memorable event. We had plenty of food, and we were able to continue the long-standing tradition of inviting my father's older aunts and uncles for the holiday dinner. During the New Year's party at Uncle Paul's home on the second floor of the buildidng, six of us children participated in a Christmas pageant—the boys were shepherds, the girls were angels. The newborn cousin, Géza, was placed in the manger as baby Jesus.

Quite early in the winter of 1946, my mother, Aunt Margó, and Aunt Ilike decided the nine Csonka children should learn to dance and enrolled us in Mimi *néni*'s dancing school at Gerlóczy Street in Pest. (My mother herself was a pupil of Mimi *néni*'s in the 1920s.) To get to the school from Buda where we lived, we had to cross the Danube. But with all of the bridges sadly hanging in the river, we had to board a small outboard motorboat called the Monitor to be ferried across by Russian soldiers. We were packed like sardines in the flimsy little boat while huge chunks of ice floated around us in the river. I felt positively nauseated by the thought of taking the

Monitor to get across the Danube. I was in second grade at this time. I had no social skills of any sort, and I certainly did not relish the idea of learning how to dance with awkward boys, who had sweaty palms. Nevertheless, I went along because my family decided that dancing would be good for all Csonka children.

The year 1946 brought about tremendous changes in the Hungarian economy. There was runaway inflation after the war, and the new Hungarian government instituted a monetary reform. On August 20, 1946, the new currency, the "forint," was introduced, which replaced the "pengő," the old currency. This change symbolized the official end of the old regime.

In this year, several political parties emerged, competing with one another for political power. The Social Democratic Party, the Independent Small Holder's Party, the Farmers' Party, and the Hungarian Workers' Party all appeared on the horizon. The newly reconstituted Communist Party, modeled after the Communist Party of 1917, entered the political arena. During the elections of 1947, the Communist Party received an unremarkable 22 percent of the total vote.

But the year after, 1948, was the year of the "big

turnaround." Through a carefully orchestrated coup, the Communist Party wrested the power from the hand of all competing parties and declared itself the winner of the national elections. The votes were fabricated and all opposition to Communist domination was suppressed. The emerging leaders of the new Communist Party were no strangers to the Hungarian political scene. They were all students of the "old" Stalinist school in Moscow and had spent considerable time in the Soviet Union during the emergence of the Soviet system.

The two chief leading personalities of the Hungarian Communist Party of 1948 were Mátyás Rákosi, president of the ministerial council, and Ernő Gerő, minister of the interior. These two men surrounded themselves with their political allies, chief among them being Péter Gábor, the director of the Hungarian Security Police (ÁVO). With one stroke, the leaders established a Soviet-style totalitarian state, in which a one party-system became dominant. The leaders of the previous political parties were eliminated. Marshall Tito, a former political associate, was declared a dissident.

In this year of the turnaround, the Hungarian Communist Party showed raw power in destroying the pre-war class system of the country. Former leaders of the middle class were dismissed from their positions. Intellectuals and members of the bourgeoisie were mistrusted. Aristocrats and wealthy industrialists were considered "enemies of the people." The full power of the government was placed into the hands of the Communists, who came from working-class or peasant families.

The symbol "X" was placed next to the name of anyone in Hungarian society who was an enemy of the Communist system; in essence it was political profiling. A child coming from a family with an X label was automatically banned from higher education. An adult with an X next to his or her name had no prospect of job promotion in a society hostile to this status.

By June 1948 the Communists had introduced the Soviet educational system in Hungary. The Russian language became compulsory, while German and English were eliminated. General textbooks for children of all ages reflected the communist ideology.

All religious orders in Hungary were dissolved. Priests, nuns, and other religious people were dismissed from their positions. Cardinal József Mindszenty, a strong opponent of Nazism and later of communism, was imprisoned, tortured, and condemned for life.

The Communists' goal was to eliminate private property held by individuals. They declared that anyone who employed more than two people was a "capitalist." The Communist government nationalized all banks, factories, and privately owned businesses—large or small. In May, the Csonka Machine Factory, which employed over a thousand workers, was nationalized. The nationalization of the factory dealt a horrendous blow to the entire Csonka family. On May 20, 1948, my father and my uncle Béla were officially escorted out of the plant. They were not even allowed to take their attaché cases with them. They had to leave behind their factory—their joy and pride—and the source of their families' income.

The Communists instructed my father's secretary to draft a letter ordering my father and Uncle Béla to appear at the notorious ÁVO (Államvédelmi Osztály) headquarters at Andrássy Street 60 in Pest on May 22. (ÁVO was the state security agency, modeled after the Soviet KGB). My father's secretary was told to mail this letter immediately. But, because she was loyal to my father and uncle—and no friend of the Communists—she called my mother and Aunt Ilike (Uncle Béla's wife) about the content of the letter before mailing it. The two women immediately recognized the terrible danger of the possible and probable imprisonment of their husbands. The men were on the black list of the Communists, not only because they were capitalists, but also because they were part of the anti-communist movement led by Cardinal Mindszenty.

My mother and aunt acted quickly and in unison. They said nothing about the damning letter to anyone, even to their own children. Realizing the danger was too great for the men to stay in Hungary, they urged their husbands to leave the country immediately. They packed three pairs of socks and a change of underwear for the men. My mother sewed a one-hundred-dollar bill into the visor of my father's cap. With no packages to carry and no good-byes to children and family, the two men left Budapest in utmost secrecy.

Aunt Mária, now living alone since Grandma Csonka's death in December 1946, decided to join her brothers in their escape from Hungary. The three of them took the train from Budapest to Győr in western Hungary. They stayed with relatives in Győr who found them a guide (for a lot of money), a man who took fleeing Hungarians secretly across the border near Sopron directly to Austria.

The crossing into this section of the border, known as "no man's land," was very difficult for my father, uncle, and aunt. Fortunately there were no land mines laid down yet in this area in May 1948, but they did have to walk in the slippery bed of a small brook so as to hide their bodily scents from the noses of bloodhounds employed by the border-crossing guards. There were many moments of anxiety and uncertainty, including a fall by Aunt Mária into the brook. However, with soaking wet clothing and shoes, the three of them arrived safely on Austrian soil. Exhausted, they lay down in a small clearing of the forest, immediately falling asleep. In the early morning when they woke up, the sun was shining and birds were singing all around them. They were delirious with joy about having arrived in the "free world"!

Yet, their hearts were aching because they had to leave behind their families and their homeland. Especially saddened about the abrupt departure from Hungary was my father, who had to leave behind his new baby boy, little Laci (László Miklós Tádé Csonka) who was a mere eleven months old at the time. Laci, the youngest of the Csonka grandchildren, had been born on June 16, 1947, in Budapest. My parents welcomed him with open arms. He was a cheerful baby who became the favorite of all who knew him. Unfortunately, Laci was too young to realize the departure of his dad, and his dad would not get to know Laci until he was almost a teenager.

My mother, who planned to escape from Hungary while the road to Austria was still open, did not dare take the chance of crossing the border with an eleven-month-old baby in her arms. So, my family had to face up to a separation that lasted a long and difficult eleven years. And, in the most surprising way, it was the cheerful, bubbly personality of little Laci that brought hope and laughter into my mother's life during the darkest days of Communist oppression. Mother was able to face up to the most impossible political situations because she had a delightful little "guy" by her side.

Alone

May 1948. How could two mothers—both with babies and three other children who lived parallel lives in their apartments at Béla Bartók Street 31—fend off the dangers that were lurking at them from the Communist authorities who had chased their husbands away? The dangers that surrounded these two mothers grew symbolically into a mythical being like a hydra, a voracious beast with seven heads, trying to destroy them. Any time my mother or Aunt Ilike tried to cut off one head of the hydra, another head grew in its place.

Fortunately, Uncle Paul and his wife, Aunt Margó, who lived on the second floor of our building, were there to shield the two women from the Communist authorities. Uncle Paul was a wonderful protector. He gave the two women advice and often gave them money when they needed it. And the monetary needs became bigger and bigger as the weeks and months passed following the two husbands' departures. Also, a great number of people, all former friends of the two exiled Csonka brothers, came forward and secretly gave money to Uncle Paul to help out the "two mothers" in the hour of their need.

With no real income since the nationalization of the Csonka factory, my mother and Aunt Ilike had to sell many of their valuables, including the very expensive Swedish steel drill-heads that had been purchased for the factory but had not been surrendered to the new administration of the plant.

The years 1948–51 were very dark years for the two mothers, who tried to supervise the growth of their children, each without the presence of a father. My brother John, age fifteen at this time, became a real challenge to my mother. He was argumentative and prone to violent outbursts. At times he acted in bizarre ways, always ready to aggravate my mother. For instance, one day she asked John to bring talcum powder to the bathroom, where she was bathing one-year-old Laci. John did go to the fourth room of our apartment, grabbed the talcum powder, and then proceeded to sprinkle it on the floor, all along the four large rooms in the apartment until he reached the bathroom at the far end.

My mother, as bold and decisive as she was in other demanding circumstances, was clueless as to how to discipline her older son in the absence of her husband. She turned to Grandma Simon, who now lived in the same building with us. Grandmother gave her a thin, flexible bamboo stick, which she called the Spanish cane. My mother never hit John with the cane but placed it on the top of our curio cabinet. When John started acting up, my mother went to the cabinet and began rattling the cane with her outstretched arm. This was usually enough to settle my brother down.

How did my young mother and Aunt Ilike fare financially during these hard times? First of all, they got word from the Austrian Embassy in Budapest that both husbands arrived safely in Austria. They also learned that my father and Uncle Béla had found employment as mechanical engineers in Salzburg. The two men were hired to build military barracks for the U.S. troops stationed in the area, and they were paid in American dollars for their work. Slowly, very slowly, after a year had passed, we began to receive short letters from Austria in the regular mail. My father signed his new name: "Peter Nagy" on the outside of the envelope. In just a few words, he indicated that he was fine, and he sent us his love. In turn, my mother wrote short letters to Peter Nagy, likewise telling him that we were fine, and that we sent him our love.

Soon, my father and uncle found a way to help us financially in Budapest. They contacted a Hungarian government-controlled business company, IKKA (IBUSZ Külföldi Kereskedelmi Akció), which charged a lot of money in exchange for providing goods and services to the relatives of exiles in Hungary. Through IKKA, which meant Business Establishment for

International Trade Transactions, we received very valuable items such as tea, coffee, cocoa, knitting wool, textiles, clothing, shoes, and even bicycles. All these items were delivered to us legally by the proper authorities. My family, in turn, sold these goods to friends and family members, who wanted to help us and knew the income from selling these items would lessen our burden.

First and foremost among the helpers who bought/sold the contents of the IKKA packages was Aunt Lili, my mother's sister, who had married Tamás Vidóczy in 1947 and had a young son, Tamás, born in 1948. Aunt Lili was an elementary teacher in our neighborhood school. Her numerous faculty member friends and their families were the primary buyers of the IKKA goods. The faculty members bought a couple of decagrams of coffee, tea, and cocoa for reasonable prices at a time when these products were virtually unavailable in Communist Hungary for the general public. My mother and Aunt Ilike shared the income that was generated from the IKKA sales. The two women, in turn, sent messages of gratitude to all those people who helped them in the days of their quiet desperation.

And even when my own family (mother and four children) was deported to Mezőberény in 1951, the owner of a small plumbing and heating company who was a friend and admirer of my father really wanted to help John Csonka's family in a special way. He sent a large and heavy wicker basket in which we found about forty charcoal briquettes, which proved to be very helpful in heating our chilly room during the brutally cold winter of 1952. Imagine our pleasant surprise when under the briquettes, we found, carefully wrapped, four long authentic Hungarian Herz salami sausages (a luxury product with a tremendously high price in Communist Hungary). John and I made our daily sandwiches with this salami—with a slice of green pepper on top—when we went out working in the fields. You can imagine that our fellow deportee workers, looking at the two of us eating salami, became really jealous. "Boy, the Csonkas must be unbelievably rich if they can eat salami for lunch every day," they must have said to each other.

Random acts of kindness, like the wicker basket, filled my mother's heart with hope and optimism. She realized that she was not alone: there were friends and family members who did not forget us, even in the darkest days of the Communist oppression.

Hoarding

The wedding present my father gave my mother in 1934 was a piece of property in Zámoly, a rural area some seventy kilometers west of Budapest in the Transdanubian plain, which was known as a prime wheat-growing area. My mother worked out a contract with a farmer in Zámoly that was meant to be forever binding. The farmer was to plant and harvest the wheat and pay us a biyearly fee for the acreage, which was quite substantial in those days. The farmer could keep or sell the wheat, and in so doing he made a considerably good deal in this transaction for himself. We never saw the farmer, but he was reliable and prompt with his payments from 1934 through the war years and after.

In 1948, the newly formed Hungarian Communist government introduced many agricultural reforms that were modeled on the Stalinist system. The main goal was to establish *kolhoz* communities, or cooperatives, in which private ownership was eliminated. Each farmer had to give over the produce he harvested to the local *kolhoz*. This was a brutal step that made peasants as well as rich farmers into shareholders, owning nothing of value.

In April 1951, the Hungarian Communist government declared that "hoarding" of previously harvested wheat, corn, sunflower seeds, and sugar (from sugar beets) was illegal, punishable by prison sentence or, in some cases, by death. The minimum that could be kept was established by the government at five kilograms (approximately eleven pounds), a minuscule amount in any farmer's holdings. To many a farmer, such a decree meant the death knell. The farmer who was my mother's tenant was stuck with a dilemma. He had stored wheat on the property from the previous growing season (making him appear a hoarder), but he no longer could sell the wheat to local mills. What was he to do?

One nice day later that month, my mother's tenant from Zámoly showed up at our apartment on Bartók Béla Street. We had never seen this farmer before. But he brought us twenty-one heavy bags of flour, which he deposited in our entrance hallway. He claimed that he was scared of being considered a hoarder, and, as he was only a tenant, he handed over the bags of flour to my mother, the rightful owner. Then the farmer said good-bye and left.

Mother was likewise terrified. She knew she had to get rid of the sacks of flour that were now neatly stacked in our little hallway, which led from the entrance hall to our living room. The bags were covered with huge, brown pieces of tarp to hide the contents from unauthorized eyes. While my mother worried about the possibility of being labeled a hoarder herself, Grandmother Simon entered the picture. Grandma's idea was that we should quickly give away the sacks to various friends and relatives who lived in our building or in the vicinity. However, she first wanted to see the contents of the sacks. So our housekeeper Rézi dragged one very heavy sack from the corridor into the kitchen. I will never forget what I saw when my grandmother opened the sack. It was full of large worms and vermin. The sight was disgusting!

At this point, my grandmother, a brave woman, took a large, round sieve made of rough horse hair, and she began scooping the pasty, infested flour onto the drum. Then she began shaking the sieve, hoping that the vermin would stay on top and fine grains of flour would fall below into a container. But no such thing happened. After working this way for hours and hours without success, my grandmother's hair, face, eyebrows, and hands were covered with gook. She looked like a snowman. After trying her luck on another sack of flour, these efforts were likewise disappointing. My grandmother finally quit the operation, which yielded some flour but of a totally useless consistency. Since one bag after another was infested with vermin, there was nothing to be done but throw them all out.

My mother called together the family council made up of Uncle Paul, Aunt Margó, Aunt Ilike, and Aunt Lili, who lived with her husband, Uncle Tamás, in my grandmother's apartment. They all agreed that the sacks of flour must be tossed out before the governmental authorities seized them and declared my mother a hoarder. All of us felt less fearful after Rézi lugged the twenty-one sacks of flour to the curb in front of our apartment. Now my mother no longer worried about being blamed a hoarder. But there were other serious worries.

All the adults lived in dread of a house search, which had been experienced by numerous residents of Budapest and the rest of the country. And yes, the dreaded house search, indeed, happened in our home.

House Search

Immediately after the April 1951 decree by the Hungarian government regarding the illegal hoarding of food, the specter of a house search by the ÁVO, Hungary's state security agency, reared its ugly head. Members of the so-called middle class (not the farmers or the factory workers) were trembling throughout the whole country about the prospect of a search. Included in the decree was the stipulation that households were allowed only two kilograms of sugar. Doctors, lawyers, teachers, and other intellectuals found themselves in their bathrooms near the bathtub with bags of white processed sugar, which they had been saving since the war years. Now they turned on the hot water and slowly dissolved five, ten, or more kilos of sugar, down the drain.

There were false rumors, rampant at these unsettling times, about suicides by formerly wealthy property owners, who did not wish to subject their homes to house searches. They were afraid that the authorities would smear them with fabricated charges about food hoarding or, even worse, having weapons in their homes. Owning any kind of weapon in private hands was a federal crime, punishable by imprisonment or even death.

Spring in Hungary was quite cold that year, so cold that my mother often wore a thick, warm housecoat with two large pockets on the sides. In her right pocket she constantly carried our house key and in the left pocket a small index book, which was given to her by my father before he fled the country in 1948. The little book contained a complete list of the family assets. We, the four children in my family, knew about this little notebook, and we knew all too well that the information it contained was vitally important for our survival in our future life.

It was a bright, sunny May weekday morning in 1951 when three members of the ÁVO security force rang our doorbell on the third floor of the apartment house. I was not home at this point but one floor below at the home of Uncle Paul and Aunt Margó. The security officers displayed their badges and showed the search permit to my mother, who was in the apartment with John, Laci, and Judy. My mother wore her housecoat with the key in one pocket and the list of assets in the other. Shortly after the search began, the doorbell rang. My grandmother arrived from the second floor. Then the doorbell rang again. My cousin Lívia arrived to play with Judy. The security officers escorted these two people into our fourth room at the end of the apartment and forbade them to leave. By chance at this point, Aunt Margó asked me to go upstairs to the third-floor to fetch her daughter Lívia. I rang the doorbell, not knowing that the security officers were there for the house search. I was stunned. The officers escorted me into the fourth room and would not let me out. Then the doorbell rang again. Now it was cousin Mazsi looking for Lívia, her sister. Mazsi was let in and immediately escorted into the fourth room. Once again the doorbell rang and this time it was Paul, the older brother of Lívia and Mazsi. He was sent to the fourth room and was not allowed to leave.

Now, some time elapsed. We, in the fourth room, started to think this was funny. We went down on the floor and started playing a party game called Morocco with long, red-and-white painted wooden sticks. While we were outwardly laughing about the ridiculousness of the situation, inwardly we were terrified by the drama that was playing out in the rest of the apartment. What if they found the notebook in my mother's pocket? What if she was accused of hiding a weapon, or the like? What if she were to go to jail? My mother was alone with the three officers, who had also sent my two brothers and sister into the fourth room.

As the tension mounted, the doorbell rang again. Aunt Margó arrived. She was furious. She had no notion why her three children had not come down from the third floor, as she had requested. Soon enough, she found out that the house search was the reason for the delay. At this point the ÁVO officers opened the door to the fourth room letting all of us out. The officers declared that the house search was completed. They had opened all drawers and left them open; they had rummaged in the clothes closets and in the linen cabinet; they upturned the beds, looking under the mattresses, for weapons or money, I suppose. They came up empty-handed and finally left without taking any object.

Now the question: what happened to the list of assets? Well, while the officers proceeded with the search, room after room, and walked ahead of my mother, my mother—a brave woman—stayed behind, reached in her left pocket and slipped the small notebook into a big, open drawer, at the bottom of the dresser in a room already searched. This drawer, left open by the officers, was filled with the total chaos of my three-year-old brother's toys. She simply deposited this vital information there, and the officers were fooled. Victory!

As the officers departed, they handed my mother a warrant that stated that she was to appear the next morning at a given time at the notorious ÁVO headquarters at Andrássy Street 60 for further investigation. What would this mean for our family, we children wondered with great trepidation. Would our mother be arrested? Only the future would tell.

Trials and Tribulations

Yes, the very next day after the house search, my mother was summoned to the "house of terror" at Andrássy Street in Pest. Incongruous as it may seem, the headquarters of the ÁVO was located in a grand apartment building overlooking an elegant boulevard. Within could be found rooms for questioning people with suspicious associations and holding cells for prospective political prisoners, as well as torture chambers and places of execution. Many people who entered this building were never seen again. It was where my own father had been summoned in May 1948 for questioning but was let go without charges after a long, tension-filled day. When he came home that evening, my mother took him to the bathroom, stood him in the bathtub with all his clothes on, even his shoes, and hosed him down profusely. There were bedbugs in the area where he had been detained, but now the bloodsucking bugs were washed down the drain.

My mother's visit to "the house of terror" was of short duration. She had been summoned for questioning about my father's whereabouts. The authorities pretended not to know that he fled to Austria in May 1948, and my mother did not reveal his whereabouts to them. The officers did not force her for a confession of any sort nor press any charges, but simply let her come home after a frightening and grueling experience.

The night before going to Andrássy Street 60, Mother instructed John and me, the older children, to be in charge in our home. Our job was to look out for Judy and Laci for however long she was away. While she was at the ÁVO headquarters, the doorbell rang. On the threshold was one of Father's former workers with a huge brown paper bag filled with crawling freshwater crabs. He said he had caught them in one of the mountain streams in the Mátra mountains. We thanked this gentleman for his gift, but then what? What to do with thirty freshwater crabs? How should we cook them? How would we eat them?

I went from apartment to apartment, asking for suggestions on how to cook a crab. Finally, someone knew the answer: "Lift up the crab, take the middle, long, protruding tip of the crab's tail, and twist it, pulling out the vein of the animal. This twisting motion will kill the crab. Throw the crab into boiling water until it turns red. Then fish it out with a large fork, and voilà! Eat it." John volunteered to tear out the protruding middle tip of the crab's tail. This went very slowly because the crab resisted being picked up and tried to grab him with its sharp scissor-like claws. Somehow, however, my brother managed, one by one, to prepare the crabs. I stood by with a large kettle of boiling water. We invited my grandmother for dinner, which John and I alone fixed. We cracked the bony parts of the animal with the nutcrackers that we used on walnuts. The dinner was delicious: what a feast! It was after dinnertime when my mother returned from the ÁVO headquarters. She was exhausted, but still hungry for a good meal, and especially for one she did not have to prepare.

Unfortunately, nobody slept well that night. That was the day we received notification in the mail that the Hungarian government had decided to confiscate our beautiful summer home on Lake Balaton. We received this notice with great anger and sadness. The notification decreed that we were to vacate our villa, built in 1944, so it could become the police headquarters for the little resort town of Balatonszemes. The local government of Balatonszemes belonged to the authorities of the county seat, Kaposvár, some forty kilometers southwest of Lake Balaton.

Without delay, my mother took the train to Kaposvár and filed a petition for the repossession of our summer home. There were papers to sign and documents to present. Finally, she was interviewed by the authorities, and then she had to pay a hefty sum for filing the charges. But, to no avail. We no longer had the use of our villa. Meanwhile, we were left alone in the apartment for the three days that she was in Kaposvár. Although John and I were in charge, various aunts and uncles checked in on us periodically. My grandma took care of my little brother, while we older children continued to go to school during my mother's absence.

Bad News

While my mother was in Kaposvár, some terrible news was spreading throughout the city of Budapest. People were whispering: deportation, deportation, deportation. This horrible word meant that families were being evacuated from their homes and sent into exile in the countryside near the Romanian and Russian borders to the east and northeast. The ultimate destination of the deportees, we believed, was Siberia. (Those who have read the novel *Dr. Zhivago* will understand the terror experienced by families fearing deportation.)

Why was this happening? And to whom? And why not to others?

First, a short answer as to why. Someone wanted our apartment. There was a great influx of people from neighboring regions into the capital of Hungary after the war, and the Communist government needed housing for these people. The apartments of the wealthy capitalists had spacious rooms, where several families could take up lodging. Evacuating and deporting the "enemies of the people" was the perfect solution.

Who was affected? Deportation was targeting the people who fell outside the three accepted classes—worker, peasant, intellectual—in a communist society. All others were enemies of the people as I described earlier when listing the devastating changes that occurred in 1948, and as such were identified by an X on their ID cards, documents, and certificates. Under this system of political profiling, the X appeared next to our names because the Csonkas were capitalists, middle-class, dissidents, and liberals. Thus, on many fronts, we were enemies of the people in the eyes of the Soviets.

Well, you might wonder, why were the families of Béla Csonka and Paul Csonka not deported and their apartments confiscated? As a co-owner of the factory, Uncle Béla, like my father, was a capitalist. The authorities had indeed determined to deport him and his family. (Uncle Béla, of course, like my father, was in Salzburg.) But, in their haste to issue the order of deportation, the authorities made a bureaucratic error so very typical of the communist system. After consulting the phone book, they issued the order to the wrong Béla Csonka! So Aunt Ilike and her four children were spared. Dr. Paul Csonka was a different case. Uncle Paul was highly regarded in two professions: architecture and academia. He was considered an expert in evaluating the weight-bearing capability of Budapest buildings that had been damaged during the war, and his academic accolades and achievements were vast. He was, as well, an outspoken critic of the Soviet system, and President Rákosi sorely wanted to remove Paul Csonka from his public positions. However, Uncle Paul kept his positions—and his apartment—in spite of Rákosi because there was no one else in the country with his expertise or who could teach the high-level specialized courses that he taught.

In three days time, some 30,000 orders of deportation were mailed to middle-class families in Budapest. Members of the Hungarian aristocracy were hit hard, but industrialists, entrepreneurs, military personnel, and white-collar workers were also singled out. People cried out in despair. The dreaded deportation slip spelled out that the deportee had to vacate his or her home within twenty-four hours and show up at a certain small village or hamlet. The Ministry of the Interior of Hungary specified on each deportation slip that the deportee was not to leave the point of destination without police approval.

From May through September of 1951, deportation slips were mailed out with frightening speed. Mondays, Wednesdays and Fridays were the days to vacate the apartment; Tuesdays, Thursdays and Saturdays were for travel to the designated village. In fact, a ditty was composed about the regularity of the deportation:

Három frász-nap,
Három gyász-nap.
Utána jön a vasárnap.

Three days of trembling
Three days of weeping
And then, Sunday is coming.

The scenario repeated itself, over and over again. The Hungarian Communist government was following the Stalinist model of forcing thousands of dissidents out of their homes. Cosmopolitan city-dwellers suddenly found themselves living in stables, pig stys, and shanties, without heat, electricity, running water, and toilet facilities. In Budapest, anyone from the liberal middle-class who had not yet been deported started packing. Everybody was afraid of the day when the deportation slip would be issued.

My mother was certain that our family would be deported. Uncle Paul, Aunt Margó, Aunt Ilike, Aunt Lili, and my grandmother suggested that we move to Balatonszemes in order to disappear from the public eye. So, we left for Balatonszemes, where we rented an apartment in the villa Pihenő, which was adjacent to our own summer home. Now we could see the policemen going in and out of our beautiful villa. What an annoying sight! I was very angry—being so close, and yet, so far away.

Our difficulties with the Communist takeover of our summer home became literally unbearable when in mid-June my brother John became gravely ill and was bedridden for weeks. John had had a rheumatic heart condition since age five. Now this disease developed into pericarditis, a life-threatening illness. Fortunately, Dr. Ödön Kiss, our physician in Balatonszemes, was able to treat him with penicillin. Soon, my father sent ACTH (adrenocorticotropic hormone), a very new medication, from the United States, which helped to stabilize John's heart condition.

During this period, I was experiencing a triple unspoken anxiety. My mother was trying to wrestle back our villa from the policemen; my brother was in bed with a serious illness; and we all worried about the possibility of deportation. I have never been so deeply depressed in my life. At night, I was praying nonstop that my brother would not die. During the day, my mother's worried face gave me added anxiety.

In the midst of these worries, on June 16, Grandmother Simon arrived from Budapest and brought the bad news. Our family had received the deportation order. The document was printed on a flimsy piece of brown paper, which read:

Destination: Mezőberény
Surrender apartment by: June 17, 1951
Day of travel: June 18, 1951

For my mother, the biggest question was: What to do about her gravely ill son? John, who could not even sit up in bed, was totally unable to travel to Mezőberény. In sheer despair she sent a telegram to Ernő Gerő, minister of the interior, asking him to postpone John's deportation for health reasons. Gerő responded immediately, and he gave us permission to leave John under the care of Uncle Paul and Aunt Margó in their villa next door in Balatonszemes.

Within half a day, so much changed in our lives. My mother, sister Judy, younger brother Laci, and myself had officially become deportees. We had to immediately abandon our rented apartment in Balatonszemes and get on the very next train to Budapest. While we were in Balatonszemes, our beautiful apartment in Budapest had been emptied by helpful family members, friends, and other relatives. They helped us by taking and storing our furniture and other possessions. Nevertheless, I felt that we would never see our belongings again.

With no place to stay that night, a friendly family, the Genthons, took us in. They lived near the Eastern Railway Station (Keleti) of Budapest, where our train was to depart early the next morning, on June 18.

And so, at the crack of dawn, we began our historic journey to our place of deportation: Mezőberény. We had no luggage. We wore the clothes we had on our backs. My mother had one little leather travel handbag with money for the days to follow. Little Laci held his favorite pillow in his arms. That was all that we possessed.

After a long ride on a slow-moving train, we arrived in Mezőberény, a sleepy farm community of some 11,400 people. The day was hot and upon arrival we had to walk on a dusty road from the railway station for about six kilometers. We had no food to eat, no water to drink, and no resting spot for our weary bodies. Our only goal was to find Hunyadi János Street 1, our future home. We all experienced a real *Dr. Zhivago* moment. We knew that our new address would be just a temporary resting place. Our final destination, we were certain, would be Siberia.

PART IV

Deportation
(June 1951-August 1953)

Mezőberény

When the four of us arrived in Mezőberény, we were surprised that 240 other Budapest families had also been deported to this town not far from the border of Romania on the Great Hungarian Plain. As soon as we found our new address at Hunyadi János Street 1, we met our landlord, János Király, a once prosperous seventy-six-year-old farmer. We called him Király *bácsi,* or Uncle Király.

Király *bácsi* was a *kulák,* one of the archenemies of the repressive Hungarian government, which modeled its persecution of wealthy landowners (*kuláks*) on the Soviet system, dictated by Stalin. Király *bácsi* had a magnificent house and huge property on one of the main streets of Mezőberény. Three of his large rooms faced the shady street and two of the rooms overlooked the inner courtyard. In the prime of his life, Király *bácsi* was a wealthy farmer, the owner of two independent farms, with modern machinery to till the fertile soil found in the southeastern county of Békés, where Mezőberény was located. He owned and slaughtered eighty pigs every year and delivered the meat to farmers in Romania (then Transylvania). He had a huge granary, stocked to the rooftop with the best quality grain, which he sold at high prices. He was an enormously rich man before the advent of communism in Hungary.

But the Communist government set out to destroy the *kulák* class by forcing farmers into Soviet-style collective farms, the *kolhoz*. The taxes levied on the *kuláks* were so outrageously high that the farmers had to sell their possessions. By the 1950s, Király *bácsi* no longer owned two farms, nor did he have cows in his stables or pigs in his stys. His one remaining horse died of malnutrition. Eventually, after we left Mezőberény, Király *bácsi* drank himself to death.

When the Hungarian Communist government placed the some 30,000 deportees into the homes of the *kuláks* in eastern Hungary, the authorities hoped to pit the two classes—the intelligentsia and the (formerly) wealthy farmers—against each other. To the greatest chagrin of the government, however, the members of the liberal, deported middle-class found an ally, not an enemy, in the dispossessed *kuláks*. These two classes shared a mutual hatred of the Marxist system, whose goal was to destroy private property and make every individual a servant to the state.

But what happened to my family when we first arrived? Király *bácsi* gave over to us one of the large rooms, with two windows, facing the street. But no furniture. For the first two nights, we slept on the floor. Király *bácsi* had a little kitchen at the end of a long courtyard in the section where the stables and the granary were. At least, we could cook a simple meal, once we found out about the outdoor market and the grocery store.

Via Hungarian Express Service, our relatives in Budapest shipped to us two bunk beds from my father's factory. With the beds came pillows, bedding, and heavy rough grey blankets. Now we had a place where we could put our heads down for the night. Soon the Budapest relatives also sent a tabletop gas stove with two burners and a gas tank for cooking. At last, life started to resemble a state of normalcy.

We also heard some encouraging news that made all of us extremely happy. My brother John, who we had left behind in Balatonszemes, started to gain strength as he recovered from his illness. We rejoiced knowing that John would join us in Mezőberény as soon as the doctor would allow him to travel.

In a totally unpredictable, ironic way, "Mezőberény" became an entirely new, formative experience for every single member of my family. All of us—former city dwellers—became stronger and more resilient in a rural environment. This experience made all of us into new beings. It looked like being deported was a blessing in disguise!

Let us look at all of us in our new roles. John was sixteen and a half at the time he re-joined his family in Mezőberény. The first born in a family of four children, John was the apple of my mother's eye. Although he was an outstanding student in school, he was an obnoxious, reticent teenager at home in Budapest. However, in Mezőberény, he became a totally new person. Realizing the gravity of our situation, he showed real leadership in standing up for his family. John rose to be a respected member among adult deportees with whom we worked in the fields because they realized how smart and capable he was. John was elected as team leader for deportees, who were much older than he was.

After John, we need to pay attention to my other brother, Laci, who was just four years old as we arrived in our new situation. By upbringing, Laci, the youngest, was somewhat overprotected by his mother and a loving grandmother. He, however, became a totally different little guy the moment he started playing in the mud in front of our house with the other little boys who had been brought up on farms. Intellectually, Laci was far above little Aduska or Rudy, or others, who soon started to regard him as their leader from the big city. Laci grew taller, became muscular and suntanned from being outdoors all the time. He was not in school yet, but he took on the role of referee in the midst of his buddies, and he could stand up and fight for his rights.

The two girls also changed in major ways by being in Mezőberény. My little sister Judy, now nine and a half, was thrown into life situations, which tested her survival skills. Judy, who had never cooked in her life, was now asked by our mother to be in charge of cooking for a sick elderly relative. On one occasion this relative inadvertently locked Judy into a cold, pitch-black pantry, but my shivering sister wasn't a captive for long. Judy began her cooking career in Mezőberény and became a master cook in later life!

And now, let us go to Maria! I also changed a lot in Mezőberény. As a thirteen year old, I outgrew all of my clothes, and began to wear my mother's and my aunt's wardrobes. Aunt Lili gave me her tennis dress and her navy shorts, and Aunt Margó (my godmother) surprised me with a beautiful sundress with a bolero jacket.

I was given the task of cooking in the little kitchen, a job that I found nearly impossible. With the exception of the gift of crabs, I had never prepared a meal before in my life, nor had I ever made a fire. Now, I had to make a fire in the little stove, not with wood but with husks of corn that burned quickly with a large flame. One day, I found myself plucking a chicken and getting dinner ready in the tiny (and very dirty) little hole we called a kitchen. On another day, my mother had to appear in the county seat of Békés. While she rode her bike to this town, she left me in charge of the partially prepared food that was meant to be dinner for that day. Not only was I learning to cook, but I also had the task of mopping up the floor after the cooking was done.

But, first and foremost, my own mother became a totally changed person in Mezőberény. Her former prestige as the wife of a factory owner was blown away. Now in a rural setting, she led the life of a farmer's wife. She, alone, was responsible for and had to stand up for her four children. And, she had to face up to the harassment she felt from the oppressive town government. She needed guts and creativity to survive these difficult years of political oppression. And she did this admirably well.

On one occasion, my mother was summoned to the Mezőberény tax assessor's office. She was requested to pay the extraordinary large sum of 10,000 forints in support of the first five-year plan of the Communist government. She bravely stood up to the Communist authorities and declared that she had no such money to give to the state. At this point, one of the town officials told her, "Go home, little woman, and take care of your children." Nobody ever bothered her again after this incident.

In stark contrast, a formerly wealthy, Jewish industrialist was also summoned to the town tall. He too was asked to contribute 10,000 forints to the five-year plan. When the industrialist found out what they asked of him, he became angry and said, indignantly, "Ten thousand forints? Why don't you ask me to give you twenty thousand forints instead?" The town authorities became furious with this man, led him into the basement of the town hall, and gave him a good beating.

The People of Mezőberény

The ethnic makeup of Mezőberény, a city of some 11,400 inhabitants, was very diverse. The original Hungarian population died out during the Turkish occupation in the sixteenth century. In the eighteenth century Empress Maria Theresa and her son, Joseph II, of Austria made efforts to re-populate the area.

The first group of resettlers that came to Mezőberény were Germans from north-central Germany, who were basically Lutheran. The second wave of settlers consisted of Slovaks from the territories north of Hungary. Also, a small number of Hungarians moved back into the area. Finally, a large number of Gypsies settled near the outskirts of town. All the prevalent ethnic groups adopted Hungarian as their language, and led a peaceful—if somewhat segregated—co-existence with their neighbors.

By 1951, however, at the time of the arrival of the deportees, the ethnic boundaries were practically nonexistent. Although there was a German church and a German well producing lukewarm water from a man-made artesian well, no other sign indicated German origin of the neighborhood except the names of some streets, such as Luther Street or Calvin Street. The so-called Slovak quarter of Mezőberény had a Slovak church and a Slovak well, which also produced warm artesian water. We Csonkas lived in the Slovak quarter, which housed the homes of the formerly richest farmers in town. The Hungarian (Calvinist) church served only a small segment of the population; the largest number of residents attended the Roman Catholic church on Main Street.

The Gypsy population lived in the poorest part of the town, near the Hungarian section. Some Gypsies were brick-makers, shaping bricks from mud and grain. Other Gypsies roamed the town looking for work that no one else wanted to do. Some found work cleaning outhouses and others carried away dead animals from farmers' properties.

On a busy market day on the main square, one could recognize the older German women by the long dresses they wore. These women were usually very friendly to their customers, always giving more of the cottage cheese or milk products than asked for. "God will repay me in heaven for being generous," was the motto these older women lived by. The Slovak women were stockier and younger looking. One or two were pretty in their shearling, hip-length winter jackets, embroidered with colorful threads, which emphasized the narrow waists of the women. There was nobody unemployed in this busy town, and the streets were perfectly safe for walking at night.

When the 240 families of deportees arrived in Mezőberény in June 1951, the local population viewed them with curiosity mixed with suspicion. Nobody knew who these deportees were or what they were going to do in this town. Most of the deported city people were without an income, and they were forced to find employment that was totally removed from their area of expertise or social status. Lawyers, politicians, newspapermen were forced to dig ditches for telephone poles; women who were trained in teaching foreign languages ended up as washerwomen. This was a sad situation and definitely several steps down from the lifestyle the deportees were accustomed to. Yet, many took jobs in the cotton fields or at construction sites. And the local population began to respect the deportees, and even admire them, because they were such good workers, doing any type of work without complaining.

But not everyone found these new surroundings easy. A large number of the deportees sent to Mezőberény came from the echelons of the high aristocracy, and these people, by and large, had a difficult time adjusting to a life of working with one's hands. They came from a life of leisure, not hard manual work, so many suffered greatly and showed little energy in coping with a new, demanding life.

Hardest hit among the deportees were the extremely old people. One lady in her eighties was given as her living quarters a small pantry with no window, no heat, and no light, unless the door was kept open in the adjacent hallway. Other deportees, some with crippling illnesses and physical handicaps, found themselves in similar situations. My mother and several other ladies organized a "meals on wheels" program for the shut-ins, who sometimes were so lonesome that it broke your heart. We children took the warm meals to these unfortunate people.

The deportees who did well during the twenty-six months of our deportation were those who were used to doing manual labor and those who were in relatively healthy physical condition. It must be noted that the Hungarian Communist authorities in Mezőberény did not force any of the deportees to work in agriculture or construction. This was not a forced labor camp. My brother John and I took up work in the fields, not because we were told to do so, but because we wanted to earn money so that we could help our mother with our family's financial needs.

One last word must be mentioned about my mother, Nelli Simon Csonka, who was put in many difficult situations during our deportation. Of all the people I knew in Mezőberény, nobody was more highly respected by the farmers, the local neighbors, and the other deportees than my mother. Everybody admired the fact that she was there, without her husband and the father of her children, raising a family of four. Even the Communist authorities gave her a lot of credit for her resilience.

Salzburg to Buffalo

While my mother, my siblings, and I began our new rural life in the summer of 1951 in Mezőberény, my father, Uncle Béla, and Aunt Mária were also making a transition. Living in Austria in the American-dominated city of Salzburg, they had good jobs and had even been granted Austrian citizenship during their three-year stay (1948–51). Nevertheless, they knew their existence in Salzburg was temporary.

Salzburg was only one hundred and fifty kilometers away from the Russian zone, which extended from the city of Linz on the Danube all the way to the Austrian-Hungarian border in the east. Looking for a country that would be far removed from Russian domination, my father and his siblings hoped to immigrate to the United States.

It so happened that they had an aunt, Vilma Boross-Pastwa, a half-sister of their mother (Jenny Winkler Csonka), who had been living in Buffalo, New York, since 1910. Aunt Vilma, a U.S. citizen, expressed the desire to sponsor my father, uncle, and aunt so that they could immigrate to the United States as political refugees from Hungary. She did everything to facilitate their applications, which included providing health insurance and finding them good-paying jobs. Thus, the road for immigration was open. In June 1951, my father, uncle, and aunt left Salzburg and immigrated to the United States, taking up residence in Buffalo. In fact, my father arrived in Buffalo at almost the same time that my mother and we children arrived in Mezőberény.

There was great joy in the Csonka family back home in Hungary when we found out that my father and his sister and brother had successfully arrived in the free world. The letter announcing their arrival in Buffalo made all of us in Mezőberény deliriously happy. We knew that my father, then fifty-four years old, was in a safe place, and we prayed that one day the rest of his family could join him in America.

Schooling

Public education in post-World War II Hungary required that all pupils finish the primary grades, one through eight. After that, two choices were offered to students: first, a two-year "technicum," with rudimentary practical training leading to jobs such as auto-mechanic, telephone operator, dietician, etc. The second choice for students in grades nine through twelve was the rigorous program of the "gymnasium" with a comprehensive maturity exam at the end of twelfth grade. By its highly selective, competitive nature, the gymnasium route was available only to a select few, or about 10 percent of the entire country's student population.

Through a new Communist governmental decree passed in the "year of the turnaround," 1948, enrollment in a gymnasium was denied to any pupil who came from the reactionary middle-class of Hungarian society. As eighth-graders, the children from these families had an X affixed to their names, indicating they had been blackballed by the Stalinist educational reform. Children of doctors, lawyers, aristocrats or capitalists had no hope whatsoever of being admitted to a gymnasium. All the children in the John and Béla Csonka families were in this category because their fathers were capitalists. On the other hand, the Hungarian governmental authorities encouraged, or even pushed, the children from the working class or the peasant class to apply for admission to a gymnasium.

How did my family during those months in Mezőberény relate to the Stalinist educational reforms? First of all, my sister Judy did not have any difficulties enrolling in the fairly well-run elementary school of Mezőberény. The majority of children in her third-grade class came from the farming community of the town. But in the same class there were children of intellectuals and even aristocrats from Budapest. My sister made friends with Blanka D. and Ildikó P., two young countesses from an ancient family lineage. In a very positive educational environment, the two little countesses were not singled out or disparaged by their teachers, who, by the way, all came from the old school. Even in third grade, the teachers noticed how much better the deportee children were prepared educationally than their rural classmates.

My little brother Laci in 1951 was a preschooler, who also was not negatively affected by the new educational reforms. He just kept playing in the mud with the local children and learning a lot of swear words, which he would never have heard in the refined preschool group in Budapest. By the time Laci became a first-grader in September 1953, he was no longer a deportee. He lived in Érd, with my mother, in a blue-color neighborhood that had a school with demanding first-grade teachers.

The educational situation of my older brother John, a straight-A student, was unique. In Budapest, John was attending one of the rare private secondary schools in the capital, the Reformed Gymnasium of Lónyay Street in Pest. This was the very same school that my father and his two brothers graduated from in pre-World War I Hungary. John had finished the first two years of gymnasium as a sixteen-and-a-half-year old, shortly before the family was deported. The closest public gymnasium for students living in Mezőberény was located in Békés, some thirty kilometers away, but John was not allowed by the governmental authorities to attend it.

My own case was less onerous than that of my older brother. At the time of our deportation, I had just completed seventh grade under the supervision of a Communist homeroom teacher, who always made snide remarks about my family background and reactionary upbringing. In September 1951, I was thirteen, and three months after arriving in Mezőberény, I gloriously enrolled myself in the eighth grade of the local public school. I wore an American-made two-piece brown wool outfit with a bolero jacket, which my father sent me from Buffalo. I felt I was on the top of the world, especially after having found several wonderful deportee classmates, who became my friends for life.

I had very competent teachers, even a good Russian teacher, who was also my homeroom mother. We had a very enlightened biology teacher, who taught sex education to eighth graders, always pointing out the vulnerability of young girls who had to work on farms with rough farm boys with voracious sexual appetites. I loved my Hungarian teacher, Dr. Ilona P., who introduced world literature into my eager mind. In her class I learned about Shakespeare, Goethe, Garcia Lorca, Lope de Vega, Cervantes, Voltaire, and Balzac for the very first time in my life. For an eighth grader, this was a terrific gift, which I received from this truly dedicated teacher. Her father, as it turned out, was the Hungarian teacher of my own father in pre-World War I Budapest.

But two big, nagging questions were ever present in our lives in the winter of 1951–52. What to do with John, who did not have the opportunity to continue his studies in the third and fourth year of gymnasium? And what to do with me, after I finished the eighth grade in the Mezőberény public school system? Everyone knew about our strong desire to forge ahead in our education in spite of the political obstacles that were thrown in our way.

Both John and I were serious committed students, and we knew very well that the only way to remove the X label from our educational profiles was to become superstars—excellent, outstanding students. We felt we were being left behind by our former classmates, who were able to continue with their superior studies in Budapest while we were stalling as deportees in Mezőberény. In order to catch up with them, our great hope was to skip a grade by taking private classes.

Aunt Lili, herself a teacher, sent John and me a complete set of brand-new textbooks that covered the required course work for the grades the two of us wanted to challenge. My mother in the meantime was looking for private tutors to help us to pass the required exams, "once this crazy deportation was over." Two very strenuous years followed.

John was extremely lucky because in the room next to ours in Király *bácsi*'s mansion lived a fellow deportee, B. Lukács, a seventy-eight-year-old retired military general. Lukács *bácsi*, as we called him, was a mathematics and physics professor with a background in geography, who had taught cadets at the Military Academy of Budapest during World War I. Lukács *bácsi* had a restless mind and a terrific, charismatic personality, which allowed him to easily made friends with everyone including our totally uneducated *kulák* landlord (who believed in witches and insisted that the world was flat).

Lukács *bácsi* came forward and offered to teach my brother algebra and then higher mathematics. The two of them became fast friends and great admirers of one another. Lukács *bácsi* enjoyed John's quick wit, and John adored every single step that Lukács *bácsi* took on earth. Soon, I heard a lot about concepts such as tangent and cotangent, sinus and cosinus, secant and cosecant, as well as the logarithmic table that Lukács *bácsi* was teaching to my brother. John soaked up calculus like a sponge, and he literally learned everything from Lukács *bácsi* that he needed to pass the last two grades in math for the secondary school curriculum. Nobody could see into the future, but no doubt the math John learned from Lukács *bácsi* was invaluable during John's study of electrical engineering at the University of Buffalo, from which he graduated as valedictorian of his class in 1960.

My own education as a "home-schooled" ninth grader was supervised by another deportee, Lajos K., a young and energetic English-Hungarian teacher, who mentored my friend, Ursi N., and me. We read a lot of twentieth-century Hungarian prose and wrote book reports on the works of prominent authors from this time period. Lajos K. also taught English to John, besides working side by side with us in the fields and farms during the summer of 1952. Wanting to learn more about ancient Egypt, Greek, and Roman civilizations, Ursi and I decided to teach ourselves using history books for grade nine. Several other girlfriends joined our study group.

John and I, however, had a major educational obstacle: we could not find a Russian teacher for our level in Mezőberény. Russian is a very difficult language, but I decided to study it on my own. My goal was to pass the Russian exam in the first year of gymnasium (or ninth grade), once our involuntary deportation was ended. I will never forget the enormous amount of memorization and dictionary work as I was trying to understand chapters of Tolstoy's *War and Peace*, which were part of the Russian curriculum. Because I wanted to improve my appreciation of the Russian language, I went to the Mezőberény public library on several occasions in 1952–53. To my surprise, almost all the books there by Russian authors were in translation. I took out, and voraciously read, works by Pushkin, Gogol, Turgenev,

Gorki, and others. Although I also borrowed *War and Peace,* I never finished reading it, because I found it boring for a fourteen-year old. Needless to say, the works of Dostoyevski were not among the holdings of the little library, which featured only works by Russian authors who were politically correct in the eyes of the Soviet authorities.

Long winter evenings were spent with reading, studying, and listening to the Communist radio of Budapest. In the public radio broadcasts, my awareness of classical dramas and entertaining theatrical pieces, such as *Pygmalion* and *Cyrano de Bergerac* grew considerably.

One educational opportunity that presented itself for those long winter evenings in Mezőberény deserves particular mention. Another neighbor and fellow deportee in Király *bácsi*'s house was H. Anti *bácsi,* a former military officer. Anti *bácsi,* as we called him, began to teach us kids how to play bridge. In the winter of 1952 I spent many an evening in Anti *bácsi*'s living room, sitting at a table under a bright chandelier, learning the rules for bidding and trick-taking. Our group of four—Anti *bácsi,* his young daughter by the name of Babus H., John, and myself—stayed and played together for a whole year. My early years of playing bridge helped me as a college student in Buffalo, and is still a part of my educational experience today, when I play bridge as a senior citizen with my friends.

Death of Stalin and Renewed Educational Opportunities

After the endlessly long, cold winter of 1952, the likewise brutally cold spring of 1953 followed. Nobody even dared dream that a ray of hope might appear on the horizon for the deported families in Mezőberény.

Joseph Stalin died on March 3, 1953, in Moscow. The news of his death, broadcast by the Hungarian Communist radio, filled us with great joy and a feeling of high expectation. Those of us in Mezőberény, like so many of the other 30,000 deportees throughout the country, were almost sure that as a consequence of Stalin's death we would not be shipped to a work camp in Siberia.

Following Stalin's death, there were many sudden changes in the political system of the Soviet Union. Nikita Khrushchev, an outspoken anti-Stalinist, reorganized the Soviet cabinet. Many of the former hardliners of the

Moscow government were removed by Khrushchev's purges. Hungary's government also reflected the changes dictated by the new Soviet government. The Stalinist Mátyás Rákosi, Hungary's previous head of state, was ousted. Imre Nagy, an economics professor and formerly a Communist member of the Hungarian parliament, became the head of state. By a historically important decree, in June 1953, Imre Nagy lifted the Order of Deportation so that all the 30,000 Hungarian deportees became free. We, the Mezőberény deportees, were delirious with joy. We were dancing and singing a glorious "Te Deum."

The lifting of the deportation decree gave a tremendous impetus to my brother and me. We no longer took summer jobs in the fields. Instead, we focused on our secondary school studies because we now had real hope for returning to Budapest and challenging the exams so that we could skip a grade.

In August 1953, John and I said good-bye to Mezőberény. The Hungarian government allowed formerly deported students under eighteen years of age to return to Budapest if a gymnasium would allow them to register. And, indeed, John was admitted to the all-boy József Attila Gimnázium in Buda. He was given the opportunity to take private exams in five subjects—Hungarian, mathematics, physics, Russian, and history. He passed the exams with flying colors and was allowed to skip a grade. Victory!

I also was allowed to enter a gymnasium in the fall of 1953. This school was the Franciscan gymnasium at Szentendre. Not only did I passionately hate this school, I had to commute by a local train for three hours every day to get to and from it. Luckily, by October, Aunt Margó found a closer place for me to study: the prestigious Veress Pálné Gimnázium in Pest. Unfortunately, I hated this school also. As a deportee, entering my first year of gymnasium, I found no friendly face around me. School was a dreadfully boring place, where the stiff competition between students made the educational atmosphere unbearable. Again, I was a top student and earned my classmates admiration, but not their love.

By my second year of gymnasium, I was changing schools again. In September 1954, I registered myself at Margit Kaffka Gimnázium, a wonderfully great school near my home in Buda. This was the school from which I graduated summa cum laude in 1957, just a couple of months after the Hungarian Revolution of 1956. And, in this school, I met wonderful teachers, students, and loving friends.

Field Work I

I have jumped ahead in the telling of the educational ups and downs of my youth. Now I want to backtrack and recount our nonacademic activities in Mezőberény, beginning with summer 1951 shortly after our arrival.

First, I must say the winters of 1951–52 and 1952–53 in Mezőberény found the four Csonka children busy with studying and indoor activities. The summers of 1951 and 1952, on the other hand, opened up our spirits, and helped us to find our way into the great outdoors. Being so very close to nature during those two summers literally made us different people.

Mezőberény was located on the Great Plains of Hungary, about four and a half kilometers from the Kőrös River, a tributary to the Tisza River. This was an agriculturally fertile area with wheat and sunflowers being the main crops. The low-lying flood plain of the Kőrös was full of willow trees and beautiful wild flowers. The wide bends of the lazy river with its sandy shores were an ideal spot where we, the deportees, spent many a memorable day basking in the sun.

But life in the summertime was also a time for working in the fields. In order to provide income for our family, John and I decided to join the crew of deportees who found outdoor employment—here and there and everywhere. We were young then and energetic. John's heart condition was greatly improved. We owned bicycles (Father had sent them), so we rode our bikes every day to the high dam of the Kőrös River, seven and a half kilometers away from home. This was the most idyllic, pristine environment. Pheasants, startled, flew out of the willow tree bushes as we biked past them and continued down the steep slopes of the river's dam until we came to the wetlands.

Our first summer outdoor employment was on the Canadian Willow Tree Plantation, on the far side of the Kőrös River, deep in the wetlands area. John and I worked from June to August, five days a week. We had to get up at five in the morning to make our lunch so we could start work at six. During our lunch break at noon, everybody went for a swim in the river. It was great to cool off in the water during the brutally hot summer days on the plains. At two in the afternoon, we resumed work until quitting time at four. Riding home took us exactly one hour.

The local authorities organized the sixteen deportees who signed up for the willow-branch work into one brigade consisting of younger and older members. John was elected team leader of our brigade, and he was the only one who was given a machete for cutting down the long, straight branches of the so-called Canadian willow bush. These branches, once stripped of their shiny green bark, would be used for basket weaving by blind people. While we waited for John to cut the branches and while we were performing our job, the rest of us sat on the ground in a circle formation. Sitting on the ground for an eight-hour day was very, very hard. We were all working in the scorching sun (no sunscreen lotions in those days!), and even sitting under the taller trees didn't help much because these trees don't provide much shade.

John had it worse. He had to go into the jungle of the high-growth willows, reeds, and tall grass. He cut a narrow, winding footpath leading to the area where the willow bushes grew. The air in there was impossibly sultry as no cooling wind could penetrate the thick growth. If you followed John's footpath, you might find little birds' nests suspended between the standing reeds. One time, to my amazement, I found a tiny little round yellow nest with four lovely pink field mice in it, nicely snuggling up to one another.

The question is: how did we peel the bark from the willow branch? Each team member was given a so-called willow fork that you pushed securely into the ground next to where you sat, with its pointed tip below the surface. Above the ground was the fork-like, spring-activated long handle, consisting of two parts. Holding a long willow branch in your hands, you placed it between the two prongs of the fork. With your left hand and fingers, you squeezed the two prongs together, and with your right arm, you pulled the willow branch through. The sharp edges of the fork peeled off the bark, which was greenish yellow and had a wonderful pungent smell. Once the bark fell off, you had a beautifully white, shiny wet willow branch. Only the longest, straightest branches of the Canadian willow could be used for the basket weaving. Other lesser branches had side shoots that made them unacceptable.

Each team member in our brigade skinned about five hundred long branches by the end of one day. This was hard work, and our left hand hurt because it was tightly squeezing the fork for so many hours. From the five hundred peeled branches, we needed to make four or five teepee-like bundles. First, with long strips of peeled-off green bark you tied about a hundred branches together. Then you stood these branches up like a teepee. This way the wet, freshly peeled branches could dry out overnight. We each made about five teepees, which we cordoned off with a ribbon made out of the green bark. This is how we identified the work we did for the day.

The next day, the plantation overseer came to weigh the branches and pay our salary, based on the number of teepees we had assembled and their weight. However, you could not cheat by passing on wet (and heavy) branches. All branches had to be dry (and light) before the overseer would accept the bundles for payment. Every evening, when we left for the day, a whole Indian village of teepees was left behind by the sixteen workers in our brigade. This was a most unusual sight!

Looking back, I must say that I loved working on the Canadian Willow Plantation. I enjoyed the camaraderie of our team members. They were young or old, happy or sad, but always ready to do the most difficult type of work in the beautiful setting of the Kőrös River bend, with a sense of humor. After eight hours of sitting on the ground, a middle-aged woman in our brigade exclaimed, "The soft lap of Nature is very hard, indeed."

One July morning that summer, the sky was dark and ominous. The air was sultry and hot. It looked like a storm was brewing for later in the afternoon.

As always, our brigade of sixteen pedaled out to the plantation. Just as we arrived, John's bike had a flat tire, and it made him very mad. He argued with H. Magda, who was much older and also had a quick temper; the two of them exchanged some ugly words. Soon after that, John disappeared into the jungle to do his job of cutting down the willow branches. He was obviously peeved and you could see it on his face.

Suddenly John reappeared. His left hand was bleeding profusely. In his angry state, he had accidentally cut a deep wound in his left hand with the machete. He had cut through some veins and muscles on the top side of the hand near the ring finger, middle finger, and index finger. One quick-thinking deportee applied a tourniquet to staunch the flow of blood. We all told John to bike home right away and see a doctor. Since his bike had a flat tire, I gave him my bike, and urged him to hurry home.

The storm clouds thickened in the early afternoon, and we all worried about the coming storm. Everyone knew that I was left with a useless bike with a flat tire. Two fellows with a clever idea tried to repair it. They found a large, leafy plant and stuffed it into the gaping hole in the bike's inner tube. Then they tied up the leaves with twine, working in a circular movement. This way, the big plant seemed securely fastened to the tire. The two fellows then pumped up the tire.

When the rain started to fall, we abandoned our spot under the larger trees because of our fear of thunder and lightning, and then we quickly hopped on our bikes and headed home. Our workplace was in the low-lying flood plain of the Kőrös, which meant that to return home we had to climb up high, on the dam.

I also hurried onto John's bike, only to find that after thirty feet of riding on the dam, the makeshift plug on the inner tube fell out. The twine dangled in the air. I was furious and scared at the same time. I realized that I had to give up pedaling and push the bike home, all seven and a half kilometers. Everyone in the brigade had disappeared. I was left totally alone, high on the dam, with the elements. When I reached the bridge, the rain started to fall in buckets. I was so afraid of the thunder that I could not even think of the possibility of lightning around me.

Coming down from the bridge, I had to walk past farmhouses along the road. In front of each, a vicious dog was barking. Luckily, all the dogs were on a chain. Otherwise, I thought, these monsters would have torn me to pieces. I made it back to our village in about an hour and a half. The sky continued to be as angry above me, as I was angry on the inside.

When I arrived home, John was resting in bed, sleeping. The doctor had given him a tetanus shot and stitched up his gaping wound. The injury was ugly, and it healed very slowly. For the rest of his life, John carried a permanent reminder of a frightening, stormy day.

Spring Flood

Another scary adventure featuring the Kőrös River occurred the next spring. April 1952 brought exceptionally warm weather to Mezőberény. All of us children, who had been cooped up in the house in the winter, now became deliriously happy to be outdoors again.

My sister Judy, a couple of our girlfriends, and I decided to walk to the Kőrös River. Although it was only April, we wore our bathing suits because the day was warm and we wanted to swim in the river. When we arrived at the high-lying river dam, we looked down to the flood plain. To our great surprise, we saw millions of small puddles everywhere. It was very beautiful, with the fresh green willow bushes and early spring flowers all around us. As we walked down to our favorite swimming spot on the sandy shore, we noticed that our usual "lazy river" was running very fast. It now became obvious that this was the "blue flood," bringing down melted snow from the Carpathian mountains in neighboring Romania. (A "green flood" happened only if the river was carrying the waters of a summer rainy season.)

In spite of the rushing river, the girls and I decided to go for a swim. Whoa! The water unexpectedly lifted me up and carried me down, down, past the many thick willow branches that hang into the river. This was fun. My friends were floating by effortlessly, and they obviously were having fun, too. But all of a sudden, I was thinking, "How will I get out of the racing river?" I saw the large, massive bridge ahead of me, about a kilometer downstream. I knew that there was another sandy patch past the bridge where I could come ashore. Only slightly worried, I decided to swim directly toward the bridge and not stay near the shallow shore. Boy, the water was fast! I found myself drawn directly into a whirlpool near one of the brick pillars of the bridge. This threw me into a state of panic. I could not swim out of the whirlpool, no matter how hard I tried. I desperately needed to grab on to something solid. My hands reached out to the side of the pillar, but the bricks were too slippery to latch on to. I became totally frightened thinking that I would die here, and nobody in the world would know what happened to me. The fast-running current seized me in its grip, and I was unable to relax. Finally, I gave up struggling. And this is when the river picked me up and carried me past the pillars. As I looked skyward, I noticed the huge arch of the bridge above me. This was a scary sight. But I was racing, racing again, down the river. Finally, I noticed the sandy patch on the left side, where the river watchman who operated the pumps has his little hut. I swam in that direction, and at last, totally exhausted, crawled up to the shore. I sank down on the sand, gasping for air.

Soon, my sister and our friends—who had not been pulled into a whirlpool—floated down past the pillars of the bridge to the sandy patch. We unilaterally decided that we would not do such a foolish thing again, that is, to swim in a swollen river. And, of course, my sister and I decided that we would not tell anything about our adventure to our mother.

Summer Fun

One of the most striking aspects of Mezőberény was its system of long, straight avenues with names such as Luther Street, Calvin Street, and Rákóczy Boulevard (named after the hero of Hungary's war of liberation against Austria in 1765). These beautiful, stately avenues were lined with linden trees, which produced flowers that had a peculiarly sweet fragrance.

In early summer 1952, word got around that the local pharmacy was recruiting high school students to pick the fully blooming linden flowers. The flowers and leaves were used to make linden tea, a much sought after remedy for the common cold, among other ailments. This herbal product was exported from Hungary to countries in Western Europe.

Several of my eighth-grade school friends and six deportee classmates decided to sign up to pick linden blossoms. The pharmacy provided extra-tall double ladders, which were deposited in the town square. From there, with the help of a buddy, we dragged or carried these contraptions to the lindens on neighboring avenues. The trees were audibly buzzing with bees, which were attracted to the yellow-white flowers. Climbing up the ladder was "no sweat," and then we each took one side. Although the wicker baskets for the linden blossoms were huge, it soon became obvious that each of us could pick more than one basket of flowers in an eight-hour working day. So, from time to time, our group walked to the pharmacy on the main street to empty our baskets. We climbed to the pharmacy attic where there was ample space on long tables to spread the linden flowers for drying. The entire attic smelled like heaven.

Since the pharmacy paid only a minimal wage, we soon realized that we would not become rich that summer by picking linden flowers. Besides, it was very painful to stand on the rungs of the ladder, hour after hour. We were not unhappy that the linden season lasted only three weeks. Nevertheless, it was a fun experience, standing at the top of the ladder, watching people below us. Luckily, nobody fell off the tall ladder; luckily, nobody landed in the ditch near the sidewalk; and luckily, nobody got stung by the bees, which were constantly buzzing around our ears.

Later in the summer, we, the young deportees had another experience that involved a ladder. But this time it was a long, single ladder that roofers propped against the side of farmhouses to fix gutters. This experience was unique, indeed. It showed what ingenuity eight thirteen- to sixteen-year-olds could come up with to help a fellow worker and her little sister.

It so happened that one of our co-workers from the willow tree brigade, a young countess from Transylvania by the name of Lulu K., had to babysit for her four-year-old sister, Gabika, while their mother recuperated from breast cancer surgery.

Eight of us were working on the banks of the Kőrös River and not one of us could assist with babysitting duties during our workday. Luckily, a friendly farmer's wife, living on the opposite side of the river from our work site, said she could take care of little Gabika—if we brought her to the farm. Taking Gabika across the river by bike using the bridge was out of the question. The bridge was over two kilometers away, and carrying the little girl back and forth would take too much time.

So.... somebody in our group had a brilliant idea. And, fortunately, the Kőrös was not in one of its blue or green floods but instead was just a lazy hazy river. In our bathing suits, we swam across the river to the farm. We borrowed the farmer's long, straight ladder and portaged the ladder across the river to Gabika and Lulu. Once we were on our side of the river, we sat Gabika on the flatly lying ladder in the shallow water. Then, the eight of us lined up, four on each side of the ladder, and with a coordinated motion, we portaged the child across the river to the farmer's wife. Somebody saw to it that Gabika arrived with dry feet on the other bank. Her sister then walked her to the farmhouse. At the end of our working day, the eight of us swam back across the river to retrieve Gabika in the same manner and unite her with her sister.

None of us worried that the little girl, who could not swim, would fall in the water. We came up with this potentially dangerous scheme because we were young and fearless.

The Russian Box *(Lapsó Doboz)*

There was a Russian military officer by the name of Lieutenant Lapsó, who was appointed by the Soviet post-war military government in April

1945 to become the economic-political supervisor in the Csonka factory. He was a man hated by my family because he was basically a spy, intruding in the factory's everyday operations. His name Lapsó sounds very strange in the Hungarian language, because it is so similar to the word *lapos* meaning "flat."

Gradually, everybody in the family referred to Mr. Lapsó with the name *lapos,* which we felt showed a wicked sense of humor and conveyed our disgust for his role in our affairs. Pretty soon everyone, including folks in the families of Uncle Paul and Uncle Béla, called every Russian *"lapos"* just to express our disgust with the Soviet system. The word and the name carried special significance for the Csonkas and would come in very handy some years later.

My father, living in New York, was painfully aware of the details of our deportation to Mezőberény in 1951, and he would literally have moved mountains to get his wife and four children out of Hungary.

While he and Uncle Béla lived in Buffalo, they found out about an underground operation run by Russian defectors who arranged secret rescue missions in Hungary. These men proposed that for a hefty sum of money, they would "kidnap" my mother and us children from Mezőberény. This would have been the fourth time that my father and Uncle Béla tried to rescue their respective families from beyond the Iron Curtain. Previously, there were three attempts by the International Red Cross to take us to Austria in the bottom of Red Cross vehicles. These rescue attempts cost a lot of money and, for one reason or another, they all failed.

Then, in the summer of 1952, the Russian defectors proposed to stage a surprise "kidnapping" of the John Csonka family by means of a Russian jeep. My father, again, paid a hefty sum of money to the organizers of this project, who lived in Washington, D. C. Of course, my father had to let us know when and where the "kidnapping" would take place. And, we needed to learn and use code phrases connected with the event.

In a letter from my father, he referred to the Russian jeep as the *Lapsó doboz* (or the Russian box). The letter said, "The *Lapsó doboz* will be arriving during evening hours of July 15, 1952." Reading the note, my mother immediately knew that the word *Lapsó* was connected to our hated Mr. Lapsó and therefore referred to something Russian.

Meanwhile, Uncle Paul in Budapest was notified that a Russian jeep would indeed show up at our home in Mezőberény at the aforementioned time. He, in turn, wrote to us again citing the specific date and time of the secret rescue mission.

The critical date of July 15 arrived. My mother cancelled all of our afternoon activities for the day, and we anxiously waited for the *Lapsó doboz* (alias Russian jeep), to arrive. One hour passed after another. No jeep. After it got dark outside, my mother lowered the shades on our four bedroom windows, waiting desperately for the Russian rescuers to show up. Still no jeep. By ten-thirty that night, we were chewing our nails. Nobody wanted to go to bed knowing that the rescue mission could happen any minute. Still no jeep.

Finally, by four in the morning, we realized that the rescue mission would not take place. Exhausted and terribly disappointed, we went to bed wearing our street clothes.

At the crack of dawn the next day, my mother woke us all up, to be ready in case the "kidnapping" would happen a day later. All through July 16 and 17, we sat in the ready position to jump into the jeep when it arrived. But it didn't.

Unbeknownst to us, Uncle Paul was notified that the "kidnapping" was cancelled. In turn, my uncle notified us that the *Lapsó doboz* would not be arriving at our home. In other words, the mission had failed. In truth, all of us in Mezőberény were much relieved. This rescue attempt had sounded terribly risky and ominous. What if the five of us had been intercepted at the border? What if my mother had to go to jail? Could we trust the Russian soldiers who were to have whisked us away into the "big unknown"?

Well, once again, our attempt to leave Hungary had failed. Over the eleven years of separation from my father, eleven times my mother submitted an application to the Hungarian Passport Office for an immigrant visa and passport to the United States. Eleven times her request was denied. The wives and children of John and Béla Csonka had to wait from 1948 until 1959 before the Hungarian authorities granted visas and passports to all of us who were so eager to reunite with our husbands and fathers in the free world.

Irrigation Canal

Another earning opportunity presented itself in the summer of 1952. John and I found out about a terrific summer job, on this side of the Kőrös River, near the high protective dam, some six and a half kilometers from our house. We and a couple of friends were hired by the supervisor of the local irrigation canal, which was a long and narrow system of waterways. The problem was that the canal was totally overgrown by seaweed, and the job was to get rid of the weeds. What else, exactly, was in these canals? Lots of yuck, green algae, frogs, and snakes. We did not care; our job was to clean out the clogged waterway.

We had to put on thigh-high rubber boots, which the government provided, and then step into the irrigation canal with the water reaching to our hips. We were to tear out the overgrown seaweed, slowly and methodically. The method was to reach down into the water with both hands, grab the plant, turn it with a twisting motion of your wrists, and give a good pull until the seaweed came out. We were instructed to simply throw the disgorged seaweed—which was long and winding and about three feet in length—onto the sloping banks of the canal.

We knew we had to have a plan for days when storm clouds gathered overhead and it might begin to pour with thunder and lightning. First, out of the water; next, run for shelter. Nearby we found huge concrete rings, which were to be used for building future canals. We simply crawled into these concrete rings, knowing that we were safely protected from the raging of the elements.

Overall, the skies were clear that summer, and July 1952 was very hot, hot, and hot. The noontime sun beat down on our backs with no relief from sunburn. Standing in water up to our hips felt quite refreshing, except that this was very dirty water. There were moments when the six of us friends were so sweaty and hot that we felt like submerging into the water, no matter how yucky it was. But common sense dictated not to do it; we might pick up some sorry disease.

One day, however, John was so overheated from working in the sun all day that he could no longer take it. Splash! With a quick leap, he dove in, and began swimming. All of us were laughing at his boldness—and his indiscretion. What a jerk!

Other times the six of us felt we were dying of thirst. You stand in the water, like Tantalus, and there is not a drop of water to drink. Well, we went to the other side of the canal and found an abandoned farmhouse. Near the house was an old, sunken well with a dirty bucket that was green with oxidized copper. But the bucket was full of water! Should we drink polluted water from an oxidized bucket and die? Or die of thirst? Well, polluted or not, all six of us had a drink; and, none of us died that day, of thirst or disease. But John and I thought it was something our mother did not need to know about.

Cleaning the irrigation canal was our first—and the only—job, where we were paid an hourly wage. This was new to all of us, and, basically, very entertaining. We realized that the slower we worked, the longer we would have this job to do. We rejoiced over the fact that we would get paid no matter how much, or how little, we accomplished. Therefore, we loafed around a lot.

Luckily for us, our supervisor came to check on our progress from the road on top of the dam. We could see him from below, where we were, and we could hear the motorcycle from a distance as he was approaching. Moments before the supervisor arrived, we jumped into the canal and began working at a feverish pace. The supervisor saw us working and he saw the drying seaweed on the two banks of the canal. He was pleased, and we were paid a bundle of money for our (non)efforts.

Field Work II

A new job opportunity opened up in October 1952. John and I heard that working in the rice fields, on the other side of the Kőrös River, was paying very well. This was about nine and one-half kilometers away from our home, much farther away than our other jobs had been.

Every morning at six, thirty-five deportees formed a convoy and bicycled across the bridge over the river, continuing along the top of the high protective dam. We pedaled in a line a distance apart from one another, but if one person suddenly stopped, the whole convoy had to stop and sometimes we crashed into one another.

The rice fields were in a complete irrigation system, controlled by the pumps of the administration of the Kőrös River. Each rice field was laid out on a rectangular grid and between each field was a canal that could be pumped full of water that would inundate the rice fields. By October, the flooded rectangles produced beautiful, light-green rice plants. This was the right time to harvest the rice. For working in the rice fields, the government provided rubber boots. It was necessary to wear heavy socks inside these boots because by October the temperature of the water was chilly and your feet got cold.

But, before we begin with the harvesting, I must talk about the thirty-five people who formed the convoy every morning. It was comprised of men and women from teenagers to people in their mid fifties. All came from educated homes and the adults, before deportation, had held professional jobs in fields such as law, book publishing, teaching, and the military. There were many aristocrats and intellectuals among them.

I was only fourteen at this time, but I listened to these people interact with each other, and I learned a lot. During our lunch break, we played Bar-Kochba, a party game with twenty questions. Or, some people, who had brought with them noted works of literature, read to us. Others brought joke books, which kept all of us in stitches. All in all, for a young teenager, this was a place where you could become a sophisticated person just by listening to the smart people around you.

But now, let's get back to the rice fields. First of all, each of us was given a sickle with which to cut down the rice. However, our supervisor explained that you are basically walking in water all the time, and you must be careful how you cut the rice plant. With your left hand, you grab a bunch of rice, a long-stemmed plant, just like wheat. Then, with your right hand, you make a complete turning motion with the sickle, cutting down the plant. Yet, you must be very careful that the rice kernels do not scatter from the plant itself and fall into the mud. You must cut the rice plant at a slight angle so as to create a small shelf on which to lay down the rice plant with the fine kernels of the rice on top so that it can dry out. The trick is to let the rice plant dry without losing the rice kernels. If the kernels fall into the mud, the supervisor will not pay for your work.

Therefore, you need to learn how to use the sickle correctly. This is a very tricky job, and it took me about a week to master it. Before I learned the right wrist motion, I cut my left hand exactly seventeen times with the sickle. I could not keep these wounds clean because I was standing in muddy water handling muddy plants, and some small infections occurred. They caused me lots of trouble and, for a time, constant pain. However, with the exception of one scar on my left little finger, the wounds healed and disappeared.

When you are given a starting place to work on the rice field, you notice that the rice plants are growing in a straight line within the rectangular property. Each worker on the field is given one seemingly endless long row to harvest. Your job is to stay in your row and to not stray into the row beside you, which is another worker's territory.

The work on the rice field can be tiring because you must constantly bend forward so the sickle can reach down to the plant, which is quite low. Therefore, you must be young and flexible to do this kind of work; older workers tend to end up with serious back trouble.

For lunch, you sit down on the green slope surrounding the rice field. Workers usually bring a sandwich and an apple. Nobody provides water. There are no toilets; you just hide in the bush if you have to go, hoping that people won't be looking. There is no shelter house in the event of a storm. In spite of all these inconveniences and difficulties, I enjoyed working in the rice fields. Sometimes, I would see beautiful little green frogs with shiny yellow stripes. One day, I even took one home.

We began work in the rice fields in October, but the colder November weather soon arrived. It was obvious that one cannot harvest rice when the temperature falls and the ground is frozen. I began to see little frozen lizards in the puddles next to me. Soon, ice was cracking under my feet. Finally, the harvesting season ended, and all thirty-five of us were given our walking papers. The supervisor paid us well and gave us bags of rice to take home, a bonus for a job well done.

Soon after finishing the work at the rice fields, John and I contracted work with a private farmer from Kőröstarcsa, some four and one-half kilometers west of Mezőberény. By this time, the wild November winds were howling across the plain. This farmer had a sugar beet field and needed workers to dig out all the sugar beets from his plot and pile them up in pyramidal structures on the open field.

He hired four young deportees: Count Andris P., a young aristocrat from a highly respected, old family; Éva F. J., a pretty blonde, who was somewhat in love with my brother; John, who by now had worked two full summers on all kinds of demanding agricultural jobs in spite of his previous heart troubles; and, me, Maria, who was somewhat in love with Andris in spite of the fact that he was much older than I.

The farmer's field was long and wide. John and Andris were given special hoes with which to loosen up the soil so that the large sugar beet plant could be lifted out. Éva and I were to walk behind the fellows, lift out the sugar beets two at a time, shake them and hit them against each other so that the clinging dirt would fall to the ground.

Which was harder? To loosen the packed soil or to pull the plants out of the ground? They were equally hard jobs. You began at one end of a very long row of sugar beet plants, always walking in a straight line, until you came to the end of the farmer's field, some 2,000 feet away. Then you began with a new row, on and on and on. Periodically, we stopped, collected the dirt-free beets, and threw them into a huge pile until they formed a pyramid structure. The farmer picked up the beets the next day with his cart.

Andris, John, Éva, and I were good workers, and we had fun working together. It looked like we were almost done with the harvesting when the cold November wind turned into a chilly, frosty gale and our fingers began to freeze. The sky turned dark and ominous. The farmer appeared and gave each of us burlap bags that we could put on our heads to block out the chilly winds. We kept on working.

Lo and behold, we finished the entire field! When the farmer came out to survey our work, he was very pleased. He invited us into his warm house, where he paid us and offered us a glass of wine. Heigh-ho! The wine was good! I never drank any wine like this before, and it went right to my head. All of a sudden, the four of us began to have an even better time. We fell into the big haystack at the edge of the farm, where the hay was warm and welcoming. The four of us were drunk!

The cold, dreary late afternoon had turned into a pitch-black night. The winds were howling. The four of us had to ride home to Mezőberény on our bikes on an unlit highway. As we pedaled with the traffic, large trucks on the other side of the road lit up the pavement with their strong beams. I was looking at the approaching trucks, and I was thinking, "What would happen if I would ride my bike into the headlights of one of these vehicles?" I soon came to my senses and kept biking on the right side of the road until I arrived home.

When my brother and I finally made it to our street, we were laughing, laughing, laughing. We drove our bikes directly into the deep mud in front of our house. Our mother saw us, all giddy and muddy, and asked, "What on earth is the matter with you?" This was one adventure we could not keep to ourselves. John and I answered together, "We are drunk, ha-ha-ha." And that was our last work in the fields of Mezőberény.

Andromeda and Calypso

Another vivid memory begins in summer 1952 before John and I took jobs in the irrigation canals, the rice fields, and the sugar beet fields. In the beginning of June that year, the Hungarian Communist government issued an edict that was meant to destroy all farmers who raised pigs on their farms. Pigs, of course, were of great value as prospective yielders of ham, bacon, sausage and other meat products, and with no pigs, the farmers would be financially strapped. All full-grown pigs had to be donated to the cooperatives, those farmers' unions that were modeled after the Stalinist *kolhoz* system in the Soviet Union.

Interestingly, however, the edict to give pigs to the co-ops did not apply to newborn pigs. The farmers were not allowed to keep them on their farms, but they could give the piglets away. Anybody who wanted piglets could get them from a farmer for free.

My family, city folk that we were, decided to adopt two piglets from a friendly *kulák*. My mother understood the high risk we took by adopting these darling little piglets, and one of the risks was dealing with the black market. There was a stern order that forbade us to buy feed openly from any farmer. So, we were forced to find food for the piglets on the black market. But first we had to find a friendly farmer who would let us use his empty pigsty. Once there, the pigs had to be fed a daily diet of ground up corn and a cocktail of oats and skimmed milk. John, age seventeen that summer, was appointed the chief pig feeder.

My mother named the pigs Andromeda and Calypso, but we called them, lovingly, "Dromchy" and "Lippy." They were pink, small, and very skinny, but with my brother's daily breakfast, they began to round out. They were very lovable and cheerful characters.

The Csonkas in Budapest expressed interest in a part-ownership of Andromeda. Aunt Lili, Aunt Margó and my mother decided to go one-thirds each on the cost of her feed. They also planned to share one-third of the valuable meat from the pig, once it was slaughtered. The other pig, Calypso, was adopted by the family of deported friends. Their son, Andris K., became the nighttime pig feeder.

It was quite a joy to see both pigs gain weight, rounding up a healthy potbelly as they grew up. John and Andris were truly master feeders. They mixed the cocktails of corn, oats, and milk in a big vat, and then poured the concoction into a trough, where the pigs lapped up the food with great delight.

Now comes a very important question: Where could one buy feed for the pigs on the black market? With some difficulty, my mother found a willing farmer who took the risk of selling us dried ears of corn. (Fresh corn was not good for piglets, or pigs.) She had to find another farmer who would sell us oats and skimmed milk. And we needed yet another farmer who secretly provided us with a hand-driven corn-stripping machine to separate the kernels of corn from the husks. Next, we had to grind the corn to a pulp so that it would blend with the oats and skimmed milk. Every evening we set out at dusk, like conspirators, to do the grinding and to prepare breakfast and dinner for our darlings. What a routine! And all of it illegal and risky! We took risks and the farmers took risks, although each farmer enjoyed the higher black-market prices. Everybody was happy, and kept quiet.

The next question: Why did we have to find an empty pigsty three blocks away from our home, when there was an empty pigsty on our landlord's property? If the authorities had found out that Király *bácsi,* our landlord, had two thriving pigs in his pigsty, the auctioneer would have removed the pigs away from our landlord's property, right away.

The hot and long summer on the Hungarian plain slowly came to an end. Andromeda and Calypso were big and beautiful. Only three more months of feeding and they would be ready for slaughter in November. By mid-October, my mother had found a professional butcher, Mr. Király, to do the slaughtering. We picked November 15 for the big day.

Aunt Lili, Aunt Margó, and our old babysitter, Rézi, arrived on November 14 by train from Budapest. They each brought two huge empty suitcases with them for the purpose of taking home their one-third shares of the meat products from the slaughtered pig, Andromeda.

And now comes the crux of the issue: how to get two 400-pound pigs from the friendly farmer's pigsty to our backyard pigsty? This would entail walking or driving the pigs, one by one, along a pedestrian walkway next to street houses, for three blocks. Well, Mr. Király, the butcher, had a brilliant, yet practical solution. In a nutshell: starve the pigs. He suggested that the boys not feed Dromchy and Lippy for two days before the slaughtering. On November 14, I would enter the picture.

Mr. Király told me to fill a large tin can halfway with dry corn. John would open the pigsty door for

Andromeda, holding back Calypso. Then I would begin vigorously shaking the can so that Andromeda would hear the rattling of the corn. Being very smart—and very hungry—she followed me down through the backyard and through the gate of the farmer's property. I made a left turn, hoping that Dromchy would follow me. She did. So far, so good—but this adventure was by no means easy for John and me. Immediately next to the sidewalk was the ditch, and on the other side of the ditch, the two-lane divided highway with a constant flow of cars and trucks. I was afraid that Andromeda would be distracted, walk off the sidewalk, and fall into the deep ditch. But no. She was so hungry that she continued to follow me. And following her was John with a pointed stick to nudge her on if she decided to dally. I really felt like a fourteen-year-old pied piper, being followed by a 400-pound pig instead of rats and mice.

And so we walked, or rather ambulated, with Andromeda until we reached Hunyadi János Street, where we were supposed to make a left turn. John and I hoped that we could easily take the pig through our huge garden gate, and then directly into the pigsty at the very end of the landlord's property.

We made the left turn, and I went ahead, rattling the corn. But Andromeda noticed some lovely knee-deep mud piled up in the middle of Hunyadi János Street. She stopped and, to my consternation, she decided to roll in the mud. A mud bath! She loved it, leisurely rocking back and forth, splashing the mud every which way.

I was desperate. My brother was livid. He ran ahead, opened the big green gate, and then with me, went right into the mud to push Andromeda toward the gate. I kept rattling the corn, and Dromchy finally remembered that she was hungry. She stood up from the mud, ran right after me through the gate, and my brother slammed the door. Then the two of us chased her through the ornamental garden, onto the wide paved backyard, through the back garden gate, and finally into our landlord's pigsty. Victory! John bolted the door, and I gave her all the corn from the can as a reward for the good behavior.

How should I continue? John and I had the same scenario with Calypso, who was bigger (and fatter) than Andromeda, and was initially unwilling to move. It seemed we would never get him to the sidewalk. Stubborn as he was, Calypso was also very hungry, and after a while hunger won out. He decided to follow me—until we got to the mud. There, he too enjoyed some rocking and rolling in the muck. John and I were covered head to toe with mud by the time we chased Calypso through the big garden gate. We didn't relax until Lippy found his companion in our landlord's pigsty. We rewarded both animals with a generous portion of corn pulp and oats, soaked in skimmed milk.

November 15, the big day for the butchering, arrived. Mr. Király, our butcher, hired three local farmers to scorch the hair off of the pigs after they were butchered. These farmers wore warm jackets and high, heavy boots. Each put a long knife into the side of his boot to have it handy when he needed it. Mr. Király also hired four local peasant women, all experts in sausage making, bacon cutting, and ham marinating. Their first job was to get the casings for the sausage-making machine ready. These women were ancient; they wore black babushkas and five or six black, pleated skirts layered atop one another. These peasant women worked as hard as the men.

My family woke up at four in the morning, at the crack of dawn. The sky was a deep, dark blue, with stars sparkling in the sky. It was bitterly cold. One could hear dogs barking from the distance.

At five a.m., the men got the fire for the scorching ready. Everybody assumed his get-ready position. Andromeda was let out of the pigsty first, into the paved backyard. My family stood by, and my little brother Laci, age five, carefully observed every scene, every movement, with his big, bright eyes.

After Andromeda, Calypso followed at the butcher's block. These animals gave out a big, painful scream when Mr. Király, the butcher, dipped his long, pointed knife right into their hearts. After that, the old women and the hired farmers began their work. By the afternoon, all faces were shiny with sweat. The job of scorching the skin off the pig was messy and smelly. The early winter morning was filled with the stench of burning hair.

The pigs' bellies were filled with the organs used to make liver sausage, blood sausage, and the rest. The women prepared the meat, pushed it into the casings, and tied up the sausages in pairs. Head cheese (a meat jelly, not a dairy cheese) was made from the flesh of the pigs' heads, as had been done by peasants since the Middle Ages. Shoulders of bacon were placed on spikes and, with the paired sausages, were taken to the smoking room in our landlord's main building. The smell of mustard seed, coriander, garlic, onion, and paprika filled the air.

Around midday, my family and our two aunts from Budapest were invited to the nearby home of Mrs. Király, the butcher's wife. She prepared for us a healthy vegetable soup. She then treated us to wonderful homemade donuts, which she served with her own homemade apricot jam.

The evening quickly approached. In the backyard of our landlord's house, workers cleaned up the site where the hired men and women had worked for so many hours. Before nightfall, my little brother was so tired that he fell asleep in our dear babysitter's lap. As Rézi tried to take off Laci's little boots (which, by the way, were sent from America), an old, broken kitchen knife fell out of his right boot. Little Laci was very observant. He wanted to do exactly what the farmers did!

Mice

Although the tall, stately house of our landlord, Király *bácsi* looked grand with its faux marble-faced front facade, the house itself was made of adobe. We found this out during a cold, terribly windy winter night. We were sleeping in the second room that

Király *bácsi* had given us the previous spring, and which we used as a bedroom for the five of us.

My bed was near the wall in the corner. Mother slept in a single bed across from me. John slept on the top of the bunk bed, with Judy and Laci sleeping on the lower bunk, on the opposite side of the room.

This particular night as I was trying to go to sleep, I heard some very strange noises in the wall next to me. I listened and listened. Finally, I realized it was probably a field mouse that had eaten through the adobe wall, made of straw, mud, and kernels of grain. Apparently, the mice, forced into the house by the extremely cold temperatures, had actually chewed themselves some handy little corridors in the walls. When I realized this, I was first disgusted, then scared. What if the critters ate through the thickness of the wall and came into our bedroom while we were asleep?

As I was having this thought, my sister suddenly yelled out with a loud shriek, "An animal has bitten me!" Mother turned on the light in an instant and rushed over to the bunk bed. And, behold, she saw a small, circular bite mark on Judy's hand. Judy was not crying, but was she was desperate: a mouse had bitten her! John found a big hole in the corner of the ceiling where the culprit might have entered by chewing through the wall. There was nothing we could do in the middle of the night. Everybody quieted down, and we went back to sleep.

The next morning, I woke up to a big, unpleasant surprise. Near my bed on my nightstand, I kept my nylon fishnet carry bag, which I used for taking my books to school. When I looked toward the nightstand, I had a near heart attack. The entire plastic thread, of which the bag was crocheted, was chewed into hundreds of pieces! Even the two reinforced plastic handles of the bag were demolished. The mouse that bit my sister must have crossed the room and gorged himself on my school bag. All this happened immediately next to my head as I was peacefully sleeping. What a revolting image!

Although we bought several mousetraps the next day, our mice were tough to capture. With the traps waiting for them, they stayed inside the walls day and night. Finally, when the milder weather came, the activity of the mice in the adobe walls gradually ceased.

Still, one morning my mother found mice droppings on the plastic plate that was used to cover a tall milk jug containing lard for cooking purposes.

How did a mouse crawl up the smooth sides of the jug? I will not know until my dying day.

Winter Fun

The climate of Mezőberény was very different from the climate of Budapest. While the summers in Budapest were hot, the winters were rainy, with little snow that melted by the afternoon. On the other hand, summers in Mezőberény on the Hungarian plain were long and extremely hot, and the winters were severe and long with lots of snow.

I remember one beautiful afternoon in Mezőberény in December. Much snow had fallen, but it was pretty and the air was almost pleasantly warm. There was no wind. So, my sister and I invited our friend, countess Lulu K., and her four-year-old sister, Gabika, to go for a stroll in the local park behind the Roman Catholic church. We took my five-year-old brother, Laci, with us.

The trees looked fluffy and white, and everything around us was a real winter wonderland. The air was so mild that we began to play in the snow. We rolled around, made snow angels, and began to build a snowman. Before we knew it, it was time to walk home.

Since we were in the middle of the park, we decided to walk to the edge of the forest where the meadow started. We knew this meadow from the summertime because this was where the local cattle grazed, including an awesome, fierce-looking bull, which we made every effort to avoid when we crossed the field. Then there was the deep ditch, and on the other side of it the local highway from Békés to Mezőberény. If you made a right turn on the highway, you were heading to the outskirts of the town, which was about two kilometers away.

Well, now it was winter with snow on the ground as we walked across the field. All of a sudden, the weather changed. Snow began to fall, lots and lots of it. The wind was whipping up, too, and blowing the cold snow in our faces. I took little Laci by the hand, helping him to navigate. Judy and I tied our scarves across the faces of Laci and Gabika so they would not feel the biting wind.

The weather turned even worse, and we realized we had lost our way. Knowing the territory, we were supposed to cross the meadow until we came to the ditch along the highway. But somehow, we miscalculated the distances during the blizzard, and wandered farther and farther into the open field.

Judy's face actually froze from the whipping wind, and even today her face is reddened from the frostbite she suffered.

Eventually, we literally fell into the ditch. This was, at least, a good sign, telling us that were not completely lost. We climbed out on the far side of the ditch, and, thank heavens, we felt the flat concrete of the highway under our feet. All we had to do was turn right (which we did), and search the horizon for streetlights. Even though they were very faint in the falling snow, the lights signaled that we were approaching the outskirts of the village. The snow continued wet and heavy, and the wind kept blowing the snow in our faces. This must be what the North Pole feels like, I thought.

Finally, we came to the first house at the outer edge of town, which we knew belonged to our friend, Sanyi V. We knocked on the door, and Mr. V., Sanyi's father appeared. "We are freezing. May we come in to warm up a little?" asked Judy. "Please, come in, take off your wet gloves and hats, and sit near the potbellied oven in the corner. Try to warm up a little." We all entered and did what we were told. After a half hour in the warm room, life came back into our frozen limbs.

When we had thawed out a little, we got back on the road. First, Judy, Laci, and I walked Lulu and Gabika home. When the three of us arrived at our house, our mother was thrilled to see us, but she did not show any sign of being worried. Instead, she peeled off our wet winter coats and quickly made us hot chocolate. Life started to be good again.

New Year's Eve

The end of December was quickly approaching. My mother and my grandmother Simon—visiting Mezőberény from Budapest—were invited to a party in another part of town. Two of my girlfriends and I made secret plans to throw a party for New Year's Eve.

"Yoo-hoo, we will be alone to celebrate!" we said to each other. My friend Babus H. said she had a half a bottle of caraway-seed liqueur to bring and Lulu K. indicated that she could steal a bottle of egg-liquor from her parents. As minors were served alcohol in Hungary those days, I went to the local pub on our main square and bought a liter of rum.

Boy, what a party this would be! We actually had no food to serve, other than the scones my grandma had baked for the Christmas season. There were also some traditional wrapped Christmas chocolates, hanging as decorations on our Christmas tree, which my grandma had brought from Budapest.

The party was to begin at nine. My mother and grandma left at eight. We told several friends to sneak into the house at eight-thirty. John and his friends arrived with cigarettes. My best friend, Ursi N. came. (It turned out she could not dance although she bragged to us about going to the Opera Ball in a low-cut black velvet gown. What a lie!) That night I wore a bright fire-engine red knit top with a brown skirt. I felt like a queen.

We pulled all the shades down so as to block out the sound of Yugoslav Radio, which was known to play "scandalous capitalist jazz music" such as Glenn Miller, and which the Communist authorities forbade. In fact, anyone listening to the Voice of America could easily and automatically end up in jail.

But we got bolder as the night wore on, and we played the Yugoslav station from Belgrade as loud as we could. We lowered all lights in the rooms. I began smoking, one cigarette after another. After a while, we finished all the drinks, and harvested all the chocolates from the Christmas tree.

Suddenly, someone was knocking at the window. "Oh, my God, this must be the police," I thought. But no, it was my hero, Kristóf U., and his friend, Miki G., who brought with them Aci C., a bold and somewhat cocky girl, in a very short skirt. Let the dancing begin! Everyone danced; even Laci and Judy—in their pajamas—were dancing on their beds.

A big bang from the next room got everyone's attention. Somebody on a high had turned over our dinner table. That noise and the loud music woke up Király *bácsi* in the next room. He barged in wearing his long white night shirt, and he started to swear at us. He yelled, "Everybody go home." Yes, the party was over. All guests went home, and we cleaned up the mess.

At one-thirty, my mother and grandma appeared at the door. The air was so smoke-filled that you could choke. They knew right away what happened. They opened all the windows to get rid of the smoke, and my grandmother began to yell at me, "What kind of a Catholic, carefully brought up girl are you? Shame on you! Anyway, how many cigarettes did you smoke?" "Eleven," I said. Although I was thoroughly chastised, nobody yelled at John for bringing the cigarettes into the house!

On New Year's Day, I woke up with a terrible hangover. And that was the last time I smoked cigarettes.

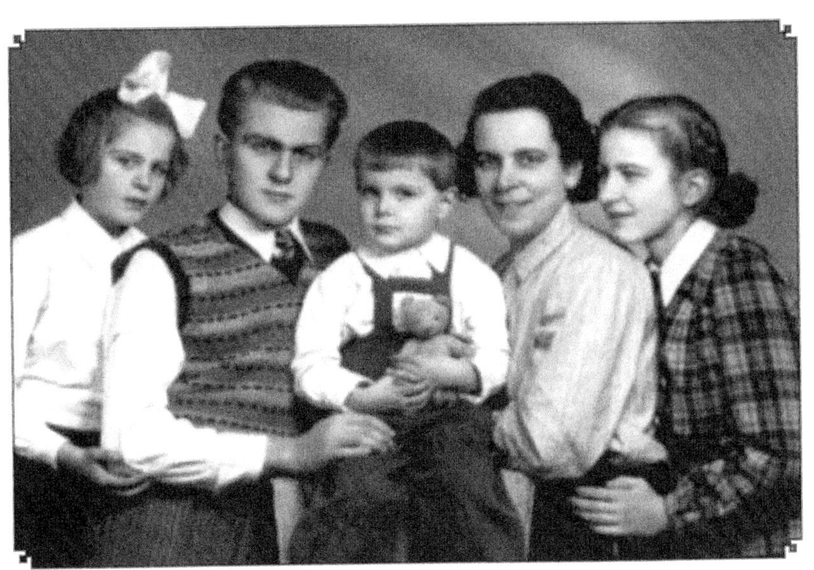

The only photograph from Mezőberény. Deportees Judy, John, Laci, Mother, Maria. Winter, 1952

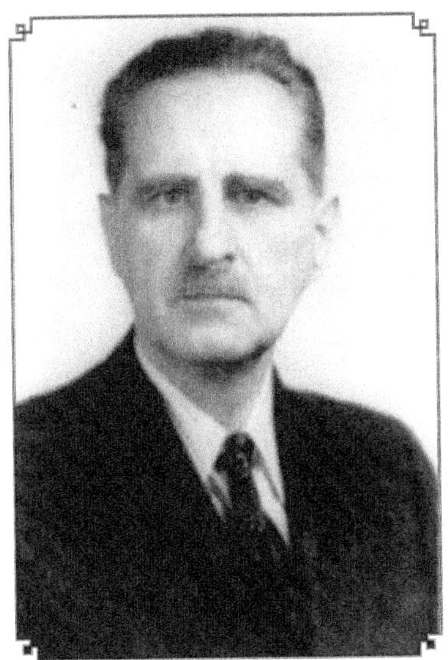

My father, John Csonka, without his family. Buffalo, 1955

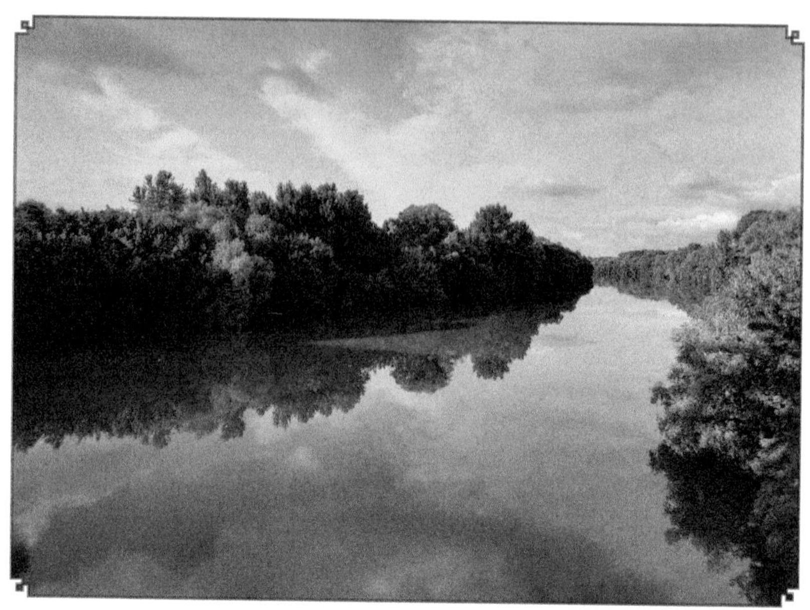

Kőrös River

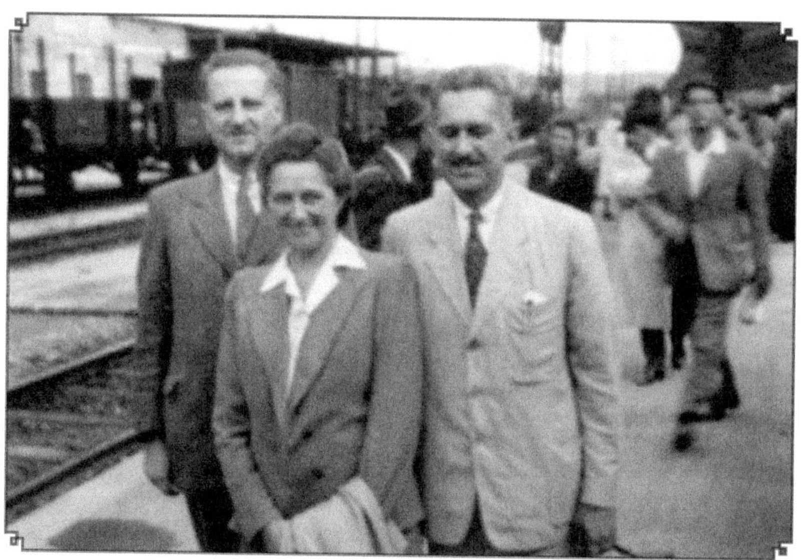

Railway Station. My father, Aunt Mária, Uncle Béla.
Salzburg, Austria, 1949

PART V

Back to Budapest

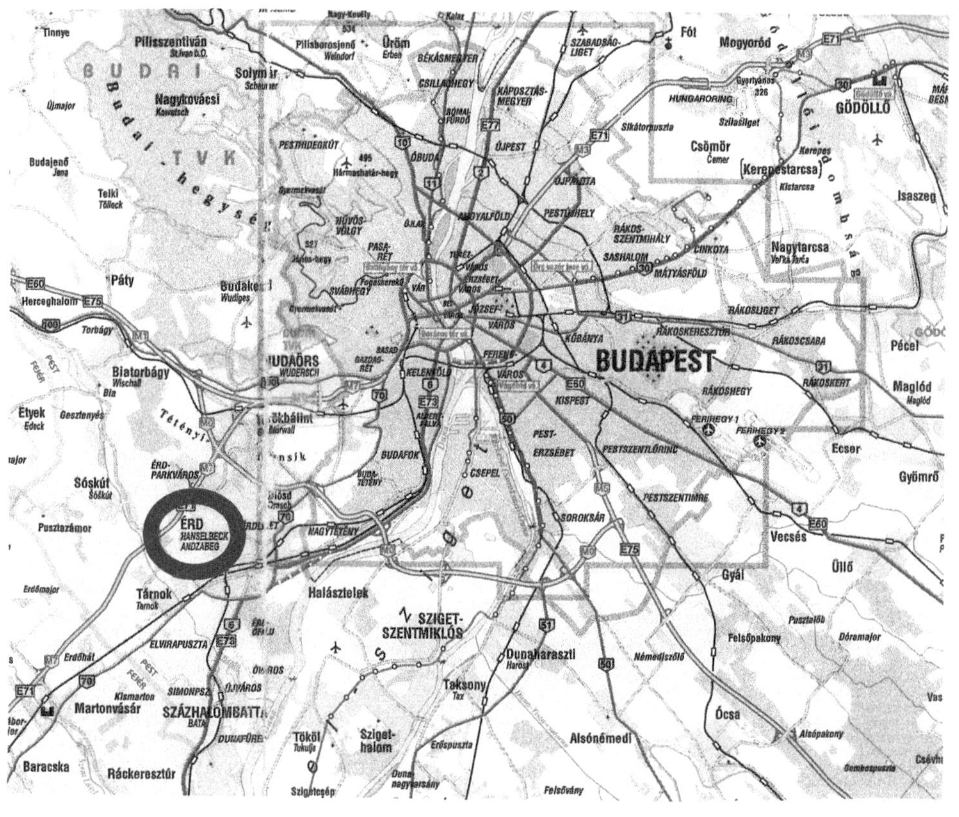
BUDAPEST
ÉRD
HANSELBECK
ANDZABEG
Pilisszentiván
Solymár
Nagykovácsi
Budajenő
Telki
Páty
Herceghalom
Biatorbágy
Etyek
Sóskút
Pusztazámor
Tárnok
Martonvásár
Baracska
Ráckeresztúr
Százhalombatta
Budakeszi
Budaörs
Törökbálint
Érd-Parkváros
Halásztelek
Szigetszentmiklós
Szigethalom
Tököl
Taksony
Dunaharaszti
Alsónémedi
Ócsa
Gyál
Vecsés
Üllő
Ecser
Gyömrő
Maglód
Pécel
Isaszeg
Nagytarcsa
Kerepestarcsa
Csömör
Mogyoród
Fót
Gödöllő
Üröm
Óbuda
Újpest
Csepel
Kispest
Pesterzsébet
Pestszentlőrinc
Pestszentimre
Soroksár
Budafok
Nagytétény
Rákosszentmihály
Rákoskeresztúr
Rákoscsaba
Rákoshegy
Sashalom
Mátyásföld
Cinkota
Kőbánya
Hungaroring
Ferihegy 1
Ferihegy 2

Budapest and Érd

When John and I left Mezőberény in August 1953, we were free to go back to the capital. As happy as we were, little did we realize the stresses we would experience as "ex-deportees" in Budapest.

Although we both were under eighteen years of age, and we both were officially accepted by a high school in Budapest, we had great difficulties obtaining our official residency papers as newcomers in the capital.

For both John and myself, the police required a certificate of residency to be obtained at the post office and filled out with our personal data. The trouble was that neither John nor I had a legal residence. Although Aunt Lili and Uncle Tamás, who lived with Grandmother Simon on the second floor of the family apartment house at Béla Bartók Street 31, were willing to take me in, they were forbidden to do so. In a special decree, the Communist authorities forbade any resident of Budapest to officially allow a young "deportee" to live in his or her household.

Aunt Lili and Uncle Tamás opened their home to me with the understanding that my legal residence should be in another location. This allowed me to live with them and my grandmother, but not officially. John, similarly, was invited to live with Aunt Ilike on the first floor of the building, but it could not be considered his legal residence.

Therefore, John and I were in a difficult situation and desperately needed somebody who would allow us to use his or her name and address on our respective certificates of residency. And, by the grace of God, such a person appeared in our lives at this moment of great need. This person (God bless him!) was Mr. Sz., a former employee of my father, a blue-collar worker who lived in Budaörs, outside of metropolitan Budapest. He declared that he was not afraid, and would allow us to put his name and address on our certificates. We were greatly relieved that our predicament had been solved. The two of us obtained the necessary forms and filled out our official residence as Calvary Street 35, Budaörs.

Of course, John and I had to find out where our new place of residence was. On a dark, dreary November night in 1953, we took bus No. 3 to Budaörs. We walked up a steep, unlit cobblestone street until we found our landlord's address. He lived in a small, shed-like farmhouse on the hillside on the right side of the road. Above was the "road to Calvary." On the top of the hill, looming above us in the dark, we saw huge representations of the three crosses of Calvary. What a miserable place for our official residence.

Then, one evening while I was with Aunt Lili and John was with Aunt Ilike, a secret message came to us. Our landlord in Budaörs warned us with these words: "Tonight, the police will raid my house. John and Maria, you better come and sleep here." So, on another dreary night we took the bus to Budaörs and our official residence at Calvary Street 35 and knocked at the door.

Our landlord showed us to two beds in a little hovel that had an unpleasant musty smell. It turned out we were taking the beds of his two tenants who were not there for the night because they were working in my father's factory. So... John and I crawled into their unmade beds and pretended that this was our home, in case the police showed up. Needless to say, we did not sleep a wink. In the middle of the night, I had to go to the outhouse, which was at the far end of the yard. The moon was shining, it was cold, and the dogs were barking in the distance. It was a bone-chilling moment. Luckily, the police raid never happened. The next morning before school, tired but relieved, John and I returned to our illegal homes on Béla Bartók Street.

While my brother and I found illegal shelter in our relatives' homes in the building we had once called home, my mother and two younger siblings were officially denied residency in Budapest. According to the police decree, any former deportee, over the age of eighteen was barred from returning to the capital. Therefore, my mother, being forty-three years of age, had to find shelter for herself and her two younger children outside of Budapest. At the time, Judy, a sixth grader, was twelve years old, and Laci, age six, was beginning first grade.

Thus, at the end of August 1953, by the grace of God, my mother found a room outside the capital in a private villa in Érd, a small town some thirty-five kilometers from Budapest. The room was owned by a former elementary school principal, whose son was working in my father's factory.

Transitioning to Érd was very difficult for my mother. Although Judy and Laci were happy in their new elementary school, my mother had to surmount many obstacles in her daily life. And they all felt very isolated and lonesome in one little rented room. Therefore, my mother decided to travel every Friday afternoon to Budapest and then return each Monday morning to Érd.

My mother packed a large canvas bag with overnight bedding and clothing for three days. Then they walked to the railway station of Érd and waited for the afternoon train to the capital. Very often the train from Érd was jam-packed, and many people were forced to stand on the platform for the hour-long ride to Budapest. Other times, the three of them had to sit on rough benches in the cattle car. Laci traveled with his favorite little pillow tied around his waist. (He could not fall asleep without this pillow.) He also tied his panda bear—a gift from my father in the U.S.—around his waist.

Every Friday, when my mother and the children arrived, Aunt Lili, Uncle Tamás, and my grandmother welcomed them with open arms. The weekend became the highlight of the whole week. Grandmother was happy to see everybody reunited under the same roof. I was happy to see my mother again. John appeared from the first floor and stayed with us for the entire three days.

Aunt Lili was a fantastic cook, and she prepared for us one wonderful dinner after another. I will never forget her Wienerschnitzel, her wonderful pastries, and her *csíkos torta,* a cake with alternating layers of vanilla and chocolate. The family sat around the dinner table until late evening simply enjoying one another's company. Laci and his five-year-old cousin, Tamás, played together, sometimes getting into a mean game of cards.

On Saturday night, every family member (that meant the eight of us) had the chance to take a warm bath. Afterwards, we went into Grandma's room, where we talked until midnight. Monday mornings, Mother and the two children returned to Érd on the early bus so that Judy and Laci could arrive at school on time.

My mother continued to live in the rented room of the villa in Érd during the years 1953, 1954, and 1955. At times during school vacations, John and I moved in with her. There was a bunk bed for the four children with John and Laci in the upper bunk, and Judy and me on the lower level. Mother slept on a daybed next to us. The five of us in a relatively small room were very crowded. We ate meals at a large table in the middle of the room, and when not eating, we shared space at the table for doing homework.

John and I missed our mother very much and felt fine only when we were with her. On our birthdays during those three years, Mother would take a train to Budapest for a half day so that we could visit our favorite bistro in downtown Pest and go shopping for clothes. In our memories, these were special days because "we had a mother again."

The severe restrictions on Budapest residency requirements for former deportees did not ease during the years 1953–55. Therefore, my mother continued to live in Érd with Judy and Laci, and continued the routine of visiting Budapest on weekends. But the next year changed everything.

The year 1956 came in with a bang. Early in January, there was a very destructive ice storm in central Hungary, followed by an earthquake south of Budapest. People were remarking that these two events meant that 1956 would be a special year. And they were right. It was the year of the Hungarian Revolution!

The political situation of the entire country had greatly improved by 1956. And the lives of the Csonka grandchildren were humming along. In September 1956, Judy, now fifteen, was accepted into the first-year program of the former Reformed Gymnasium of Lónyay Street in Pest, the same school that my father and John had attended, even though she had an X status, was a deportee, and was the daughter of a capitalist. So that she could become a full-time high school student in the capital, Judy had to leave Érd. She moved in with eighty-two-year-old Uncle Feri Simon, the brother of my mother's father, and his wife, Aunt Hedvig. They lived on the third floor of the family apartment house, in a small apartment. Judy shared one of their rooms as a student resident.

In the fall of 1954, something very special had happened. Brother John and cousin Béla were admitted to the Technical University of Budapest, because the pressure previously used against X students had eased. John enrolled in the school of electrical engineering, and Béla began his studies as an engineer. The year before, cousin Pali had entered the university system in the field of nuclear physics.

The early months of 1956 brought Hungary the "glorious spring" before the uprising. New political parties were formed. Free speech was encouraged. The radio played western music. Poets and political liberals founded the Petőfi Circle named after Sándor Petőfi, the famous poet of the 1848 revolution, who was killed on the battlefield in the defeat of the revolution and became a national hero. Members of the Petőfi Circle encouraged free expression and criticism of the notorious Rákosi regime. Mátyás Rákosi, the leader of the Hungarian Communist Party, had strictly followed the Stalinist hard line during the years 1945–56. However, with the death of Stalin in March 1953, the Communist Party of Moscow changed its tune. With the emergence of Premier Nikita Khrushchev, following Stalin's death, a number of important liberal reforms were instituted. Khrushchev's de-Stalinization policy brought about tremendous changes in the Hungarian political scene as well. With the removal of Rákosi as general secretary of the party in June 1956 by the Soviet authorities, the people of Hungary sensed "a revolution in the air."

In September, the youths of the Petőfi Circle had formulated their Twelve Points in which they expressed their wish for freedom of speech and freedom of the press. By October 23, the air was filled with glorious optimism. Mother, who arrived from Érd earlier that day, a Tuesday, said the university students on the train were bursting with enthusiasm as they sang songs in English, like "It's a Long Way to Tipperary" and "My Bonnie Lies Over the Ocean." Formerly, the singing of songs in English would have been a punishable crime. On the afternoon of the twenty-third, waiting with my mother in front of our home for the streetcar that would take her to the train station for her return to Érd, she said to me, "There is something in the air. Maria, go to the store and stock up on sugar, bread, flour, and potatoes, before something unusual happens." And, she was right. That evening the Hungarian Revolution began!

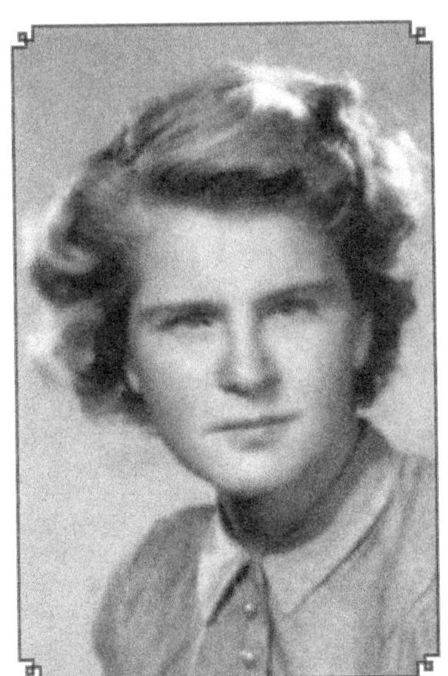

Judy Csonka, elementary school graduation. Érd, 1954

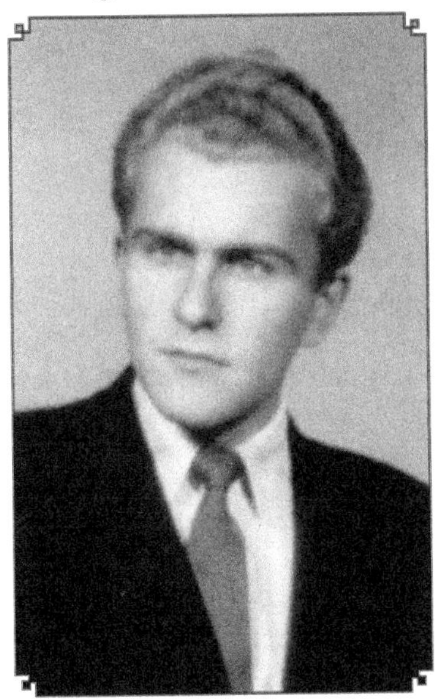

John Csonka Jr., József Attila Gimnázium graduation. Budapest, 1954

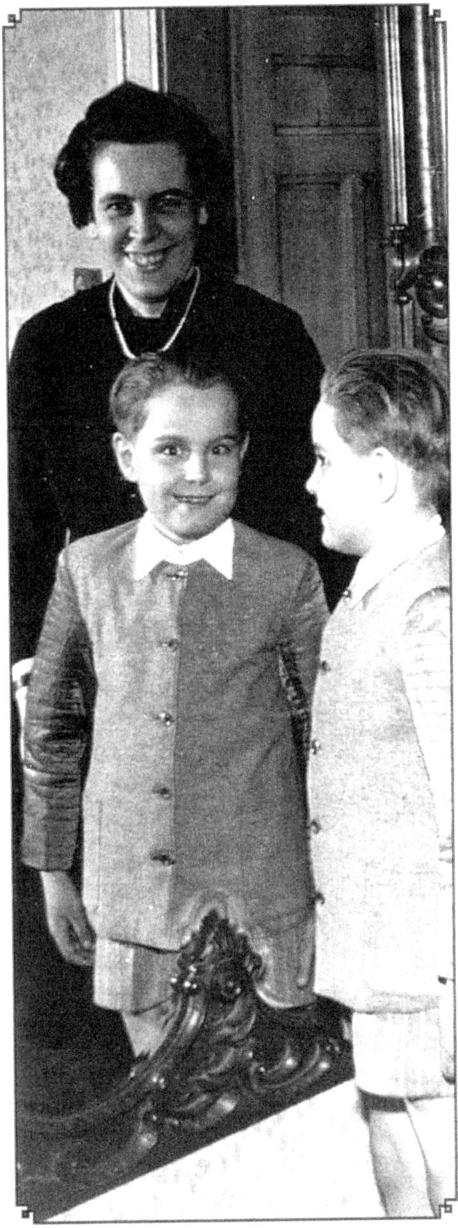

Laci Csonka and Mother at Mimi néni's *dancing school. c. 1955*

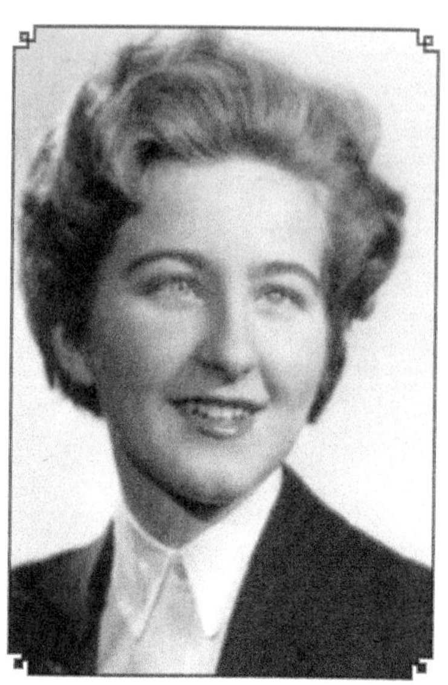

Maria Csonka, Kaffka Margit Gimnázium, graduation. Budapest, 1957

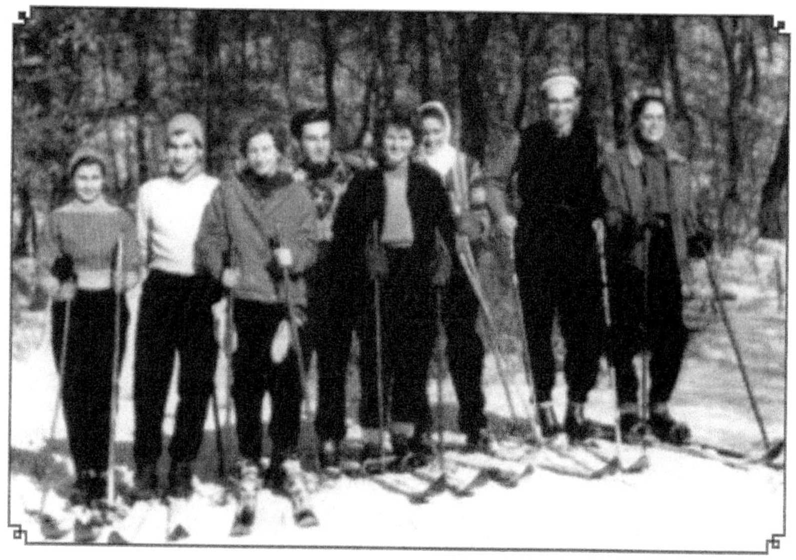

Sisters and cousins skiing, outskirts of Budapest. From left, unknown, unknown, Maria, unknown, Judy, Lívia, unknown, and Lilla. Farkastorok, 1958

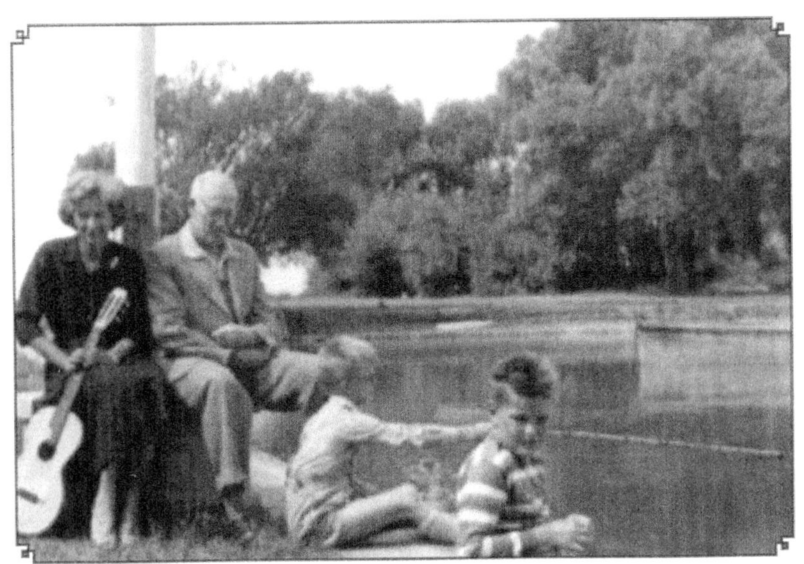

Maria, Uncle Tamás, cousin Tamás, brother Laci. Balatonszemes, 1958

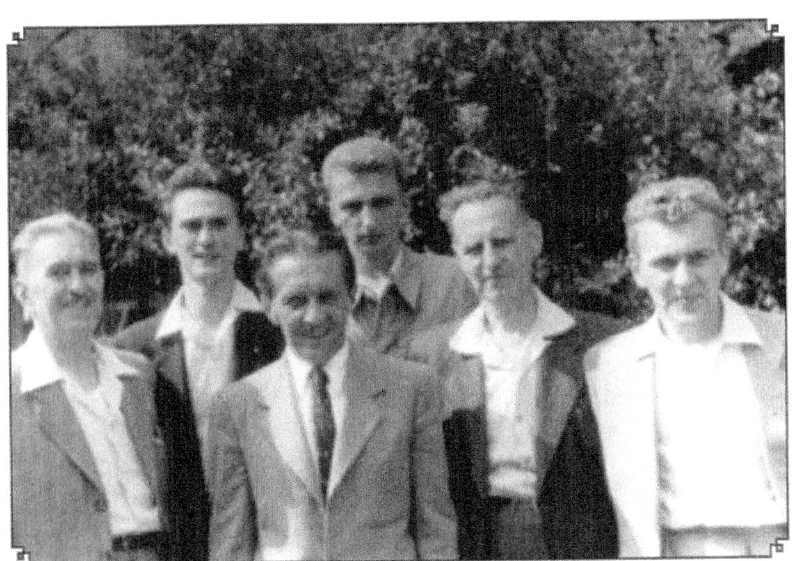

Csonka boys in Buffalo. From left: Béla Csonka, Béla Jr., (unidentified man), Paul Csonka Jr., John Csonka, John Jr. 1957

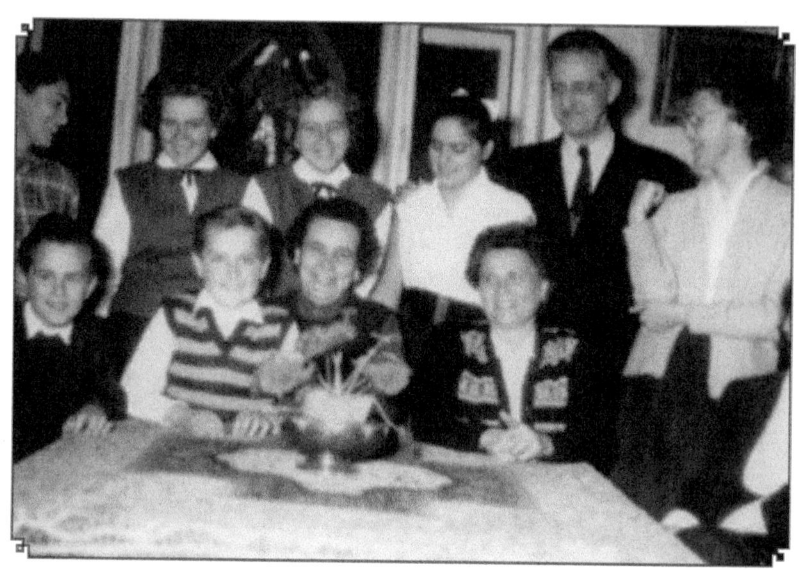

Farewell to the Csonka family. Seated, from left: Géza, Laci, Mother, Aunt Ilike; standing, from left: Lilla, Judy, Maria, Lívia, Uncle Paul, Melinda. January, 1959

The Hungarian Revolution of 1956 *(Forradalom)*

It was Tuesday evening, October 23, 1956, a balmy night, quite unusual in Budapest for that time of the year.

My brother John, cousins Paul and Béla, and their university friends had left for a meeting of the Hungarian Federation of University and College Students' Associations, at the Technical University in Buda.

That weather was so agreeable that cousin Mazsi and I went out for a stroll and found ourselves walking toward the Danube River. As we were walking and talking, several trucks loaded with young Hungarian soldiers raced past us in the middle of the road. They were singing, shouting, and waving the red-white-green Hungarian flag. They were decked out with flowers, which they received from the people in the streets who greeted them. These soldiers were jubilant, because they, as groups, stood up against the oppressive Communist regime. They had torn off the five-pointed star from their Russian-style military caps. These soldiers were siding with the rest of the country, which wanted to be out from under Soviet rule. As we walked toward the university, I experienced such a feeling of great joy that I will never forget it. There was something positive emerging; hope was in the air.

As we got closer to the center of the city, Mazsi and I saw hundreds and hundreds of university students, twenty abreast, walking in a well-organized protest march. The leaders, likewise students, carried large wreaths of green, draped with the Hungarian flag. They were heading toward the Margaret Bridge, some five kilometers away, and to the nearby square where a statue of József Bem stood. In fact, the students were demonstrating in support of recent Polish efforts to win autonomy from the Soviet Union. Bem, a national hero in Poland, was the heroic leader of Hungarian troops in the battle against the Habsburg monarchy in the Revolution of 1848.

The students placed the wreaths at the foot of the Bem statue, and in so doing they expressed their solidarity with Poland and honored the Polish people who gained some concessions following their confrontation with the Soviet military during their Polish October. At the Bem statue, student leaders read a resolution in which they demanded "sixteen points" from the Hungarian Communist government. Among the points were: freedom of speech, freedom of press, and the freeing of political prisoners. After a loud, enthusiastic demonstration in the square, the students marched across the Danube to Pest, to the Hungarian radio station in Bródy Sándor Street.

The student leaders' intention was to occupy the broadcast station and to read their sixteen demands over the air. They did not anticipate any opposition from the employees of the station, but instead they were detained. When the huge assembly outside the broadcasting station called for the students' release, shots rang out as the state security police, the ÁVO, responding with force, fired on the unarmed crowd.

The streets were very narrow and crowded. Tension and fear mounted as the demonstrators squeezed between the buildings to escape the shooting. Many students were wounded; several died in the streets. "They are killing our young people," was shouted by those not in the direct line of fire.

John, Paul, and Béla were pushed by the advancing crowd toward the radio station building. They each witnessed the violence that broke out, and each had a different story to tell about escaping it. Béla, who was very close to the actual fighting, tried to go home on a direct route across the Freedom Bridge, but he was forced to make a long detour. He crossed the Danube on the Chain Bridge and was safely home by midnight.

Paul found himself even closer to the gunfire and had to go way out of his way to avoid the state police. He crossed the Freedom Bridge, near our home, and arrived at his family's apartment by 12:30 a.m. John, likewise, was close to the shooting. He crossed the most southern bridge, the Boráros Square Bridge, but was met by hostile military units. He arrived at Aunt Ilike's apartment at 1:30 in the morning—totally exhausted.

Aunt Ilike and Aunt Margó were fully aware of the shooting at the radio station. They sat up all night, praying for the safe return of their sons. My mother, in Érd, was spared the anxiety of worrying about John. Aunt Lili and my grandmother were elated when they found out that all three of our university students made it safely back home.

That night, I was sleeping in Aunt Lili's bedroom, near the windows. Around two o'clock in the morning I woke up because I heard a loud screeching sound. I went to the window overlooking the brightly lit Béla Bartók Street. To my disbelief, I saw the first Russian tank, slowly coming down the middle of the boulevard, moving in the direction of the Danube. The tank went through the platform of the streetcar stop in front of our house. It crushed the traffic light that marked the end of the traffic island with its blue-and-white arrows on all four sides. When I saw what the tank did, how it crushed the civilian street sign, I immediately remembered what the Russians had done in Hungary in 1944–45. I became absolutely frightened, and desperate.

The next morning, Wednesday, October 24, my grandmother (in whose room I had stayed since my return from Mezőberény) turned on the radio to hear the news. It was to our great surprise and joy to realize that the Communist radio station was abolished; instead the signal of the newly formed Kossuth Rádió was heard. (Louis Kossuth was the hero of the 1848 Hungarian Revolution.) To me, this meant that the young people's attack against a most important Communist stronghold, the radio, was successful, even though people died in the process.

Wednesday, October 24, saw a full-scale, spontaneous uprising on all levels, and in all parts of Hungary. First, the Hungarian military, siding with the rebels, opened up the arsenals. Weapons were distributed to members of the working class. These people, oppressed by the unrealistic demands of the Soviet leaders for always higher standards of workmanship, shook off the chains of exploitation. The workers became the most important faction of the fighting population, opposing the Soviet system.

That morning, when I looked out the window from the second floor of our apartment, I saw a huge procession of factory workers marching in front of our building. The men at the head of the procession carried chains, saws, and blowtorches in their hands. Initially, they wanted to head up Gellért Hill. They wanted to tear down the hated Russian monument depicting Russian soldiers squeezing a giant serpent, which symbolized the conquered Germany. However, the leaders of the crowd changed the objective of their mission. Instead of the monument at the top of the hill, they headed directly to the giant statue of Joseph Stalin, which stood in a huge open square in Pest. In an earlier generation, the square was home to a beautiful cathedral, since torn down by the Communists.

The angry mob mobilized all its hatred to bring down the Stalin statue. People climbed up with ropes and chains, literally encircling the statue with a network of pulleys. Then the workers severed Stalin's body from his giant boots with blowtorches. Young and old together, with a great cooperative effort, toppled the statue of the dictator. Stalin's huge bronze head lay on the ground. Others standing around took turns taking pieces of the hated statue home—souvenirs from a monstrous dictator. Rádió Kossuth kept the public informed, blow by blow, about the destruction of the Stalin statue.

Simultaneously, a series of announcements was made by the broadcasters about the changes in Hungarian leadership after the collapse of the Communist government. The despised leaders of the Communist regime, Mátyás Rákosi and some of his associates, fled the country. They found shelter with the Moscow government. Imre Nagy, who in 1953 had taken a leadership role in instituting major liberal reforms, emerged now as the leader of the Hungarian cabinet. As the new prime minister, Nagy promised to address the Hungarian nation at the Parliament building in Pest on Thursday, October 25. The weather was still so unseasonably mild that it encouraged many people—from the capital and the suburbs—to attend the rally the next day to hear Nagy speak.

October 25 was the most tragic, most horrendous day in the history of the 1956 Hungarian Revolution. Thousands of people marched across the Danube from Buda and the industrial suburbs. They met up with students and factory workers from Pest, all congregating at the large rectangular square. On the Danube side of the square was the huge Parliament building, where Imre Nagy planned to address the people from a highly visible perch on a balcony overlooking the multitudes. On the three other sides of the square were high-rise government buildings.

Suddenly, on a beautiful October day being enjoyed by optimistic Hungarians from all walks of life, gunshots rang out in the air. Interior Minister Ernő Gerő, the hated associate of Mátyás Rákosi, gave orders to a large contingent of ÁVO officers to begin shooting into the crowd. From the rooftops of the government buildings on all three sides of the square, the ÁVO fired at the innocent throng below. A most tragic scene followed: students, workers, civilians had no place to hide from the shooters. Some ran toward the Parliament building hoping to find protection by the steps near the ornamental railings and balustrades of the building. Dozens of demonstrators, who had been targeted, were lying on the ground, bleeding. Many died on the spot.

The shooting quickly dispersed the crowds in the square. One of my high school friends, Zsébi B.-P., was among the demonstrators. She and her brother Laci were caught in the shooting. They began to run toward the Danube, but found protection only by lying down on the ground near flights of stairs.

My own cousins, Paul, Mazsi, and Lívia, were also among those waiting to hear Nagy speak. I had wanted to join them, but my grandmother forbade me to leave the house. "How would I explain to your mother, who is far away from us in Érd, that I lost you in the revolution?" my grandmother asked. And I had to listen, not wanting to cause added anxiety by disobeying her.

In a state of frustration, I went to the neighboring apartment, on the second floor, to see Aunt Margó and Uncle Paul. They were wonderful people, who had me as their dinner guest every day of the school week from August 1953 until December 1956. They had heard on the radio about the massacre at the Parliament building. They were totally distraught because they knew very well that their three children, Paul, Mazsi, and Lívia were among the throng waiting to hear Nagy. They worried and worried, not knowing whether their children were dead or alive.

"You are at fault, Margó," yelled my uncle. "You killed them. Why did you let them go?" he continued. An all-excited Aunt Margó responded with great indignation, "Pali, you know very well that I have no control over my children. They are young adults, and they do whatever they want to do, and go wherever they want to go." This is the first (and only) time I heard them argue. Aunt Margó had a very easy-going nature, not usually worrying about things that would have made other people more excited.

I left my uncle and aunt arguing and returned to the apartment, where Grandmother Simon, Aunt Lili, and Uncle Tamás lived. They too were extremely worried about the shootings at the Parliament, particularly concerned about the whereabouts of the three Csonka cousins. While we were awaiting news, Uncle Tamás and I—out of sheer nervousness—finished all twenty-three slices of apple-cherry strudel, which Aunt Lili had prepared for dessert for the entire family. Late that afternoon, our doorbell rang. It was Aunt Margó, telling us that Paul, Mazsi, and Lívia had arrived home safely. Not only the parents, but all of us relatives were greatly relieved!

Friday, October 26, came to be known as Black Friday. The whole city of Budapest and the whole country of Hungary were wrapped in black flags, remembering the dead and wounded from the massacre on the day before. Yet, street fighting between the Russian soldiers and the Hungarian "freedom fighters" continued while others rescued the wounded and buried the dead.

John, Paul, and Béla became Red Cross volunteers and helped to get the wounded by ambulance to local Budapest hospitals. The young men had to enter the most dangerous areas of street fighting to find and escort the wounded into emergency vehicles. Theirs was also the somber task of finding the dead, and taking them along with the wounded in the ambulances.

In the meantime, the fierce fighting on several locations of Buda and Pest continued. The young freedom fighters took the Hungarian flag and with a sharp knife cut out a circle in the middle of it, removing the depictions of the hammer and sickle—the hated Russian emblem. This then became known as the "flag with a hole in it," and it was the flag the revolutionaries carried as they climbed up on the barricades.

The university students, workers, and civilians tore up cobblestones from the sidewalks on the main thoroughfares of the capital and used them to build tall barricades. These young people stood on the top of the barricades, ready to throw their invention, the Molotov cocktail, into the approaching tanks. The Molotov cocktail, which was ignited gasoline in a bottle, was thrown into the cockpit of the tanks below. While the fire ignited and destroyed the interior of the tank, the Russian tank driver was burned to death in an instant.

I still remember that at one of our busiest traffic circle in Buda, named Körtér, near my home, people were kicking around the demolished skull of a Russian soldier nicknamed "the baked Russian." The intense and deeply felt hatred by the general public toward the Russian occupants of Hungary was evident from this gruesome act.

And, at the same time, the feeling of euphoria of the Hungarian people about attaining freedom, at last, just grew and grew. Everybody was rejoicing when the radio announced major concessions that the dysfunctional Hungarian government granted to the population. The spectacularly good news was: "We are winning" and "The Russians are withdrawing."

There was never-before-seen heroism that emerged during these euphoric times. And altruism. Here, there, and everywhere empty boxes were placed on the sidewalks of public roads or parks. Many, many people felt the compassion to contribute money to the families of the victims who fought for "the freedom for all." The money that was put in the boxes was left there for anybody who needed it. Not one person looted. The generous spirit of the city's population showed the idealism that sprang from the hope that the murderous Rákosi regime would soon be over.

The days of October 27, 28, 29, and 30 were hopeful days for the Hungarians in Budapest and in the rest of the country. Everybody was looking forward to the liberation of Hungary from the Soviet yoke.

Yet, street fights between the Russians and the Hungarian freedom fighters continued, particularly in the Corvin Köz (passage way) area near the busy intersection of the two main boulevards in Pest. Here, the formerly Communist Hungarian general, Paul Maléter, took up the cause of the revolutionaries. He and his Hungarian soldiers successfully averted a massive Russian attack against the large military barracks, which were under Maléter's command.

On the evening of October 31, Aunt Ilike received a surprise telephone call from the Austrian ambassador residing in Budapest. The gist was that since Uncle Béla and my father lived in Salzburg, Austria, from 1948 to 1951, they both were granted Austrian citizenship. According to law, their wives and children were given the status of Austrian citizens, as well. This meant that all of us: John, Maria, Judy, and Laci; Béla, Melinda, Lilla, and Géza; and our mothers were recognized as not only Hungarians, but Austrians, too. The ambassador informed Aunt Ilike that there would be a Red Cross convoy on November 4 that would take the families of John Csonka and Béla Csonka to Austria. He emphasized that the two mothers and their children should be at Marczibányi Square in Buda at eight a.m. sharp to join the Red Cross convoy.

Although I was happy about this opportunity, I was also sad about having to leave Hungary at a time when there was hope for a better future. But first, we had to overcome a major obstacle. Two members of my family did not live in Budapest. How could we bring my mother and Laci from Érd in time to join the convoy on November 4?

Brother John and cousin Béla had a brilliant idea. They decided to ride their bicycles from Budapest to Érd, so that they could bring Mother and Laci back to the capital. So, on November 2, the two young men, each with a light on his bike set out in the dark on Budaörs Road toward Érd, some thirty-five kilometers away. As they reached the high plateau of Tétény, the lights on both bicycles went out, and they had to ride in total darkness, which turned out not to be the misfortune it seemed at first.

They had no idea that they were riding through the heavily fortified Russian military zone with units that were encircling Budapest, ready to attack. In the darkness, they did not see the Russians, and, luckily, the Russians did not see them. John and Béla reached Érd safely and found my mother and Laci waiting for them.

The next morning, on November 3, the four of them went out to the nearby highway, hoping to hitch a ride to Budapest. A smallish truck, full of young freedom fighters stopped and took them on board, bicycles and all. My mother had to stand next to a young worker who had four hand grenades hanging from his belt. She was really worried that one of them would go off if the truck hit a pothole in the road. But nothing happened. The four Csonkas and the two bicycles made it safely back to Budapest.

Earlier in the week, from October 30 on, some highly disturbing news had been circulating in Hungary. The Russian troops, which had been visibly withdrawing from the country because of the revolution, had been ordered by Premier Khrushchev to return to Budapest. The Red Army's military units crossed the border from the east in large numbers, heading directly toward Budapest. Fear and despair paralyzed the Hungarian public. Rumors of an approaching all-round Soviet military attack against the freedom fighters of Budapest filled the air. "The Russians are coming, the Russians are coming," was again the phrase everybody repeated in the capital. Prospects of the hopeful future were crushed. The Hungarians, praying that the United States under the leadership of President Dwight Eisenhower would intervene in the Russian occupation of Hungary, gave up all hope when Eisenhower did not act. The population of Budapest had to face up to the prospect of bombs, artillery attacks, and fallout shelters.

On November 3, Judy and I went down to our building's cellar to look around and see what kind of preparations we needed to make in case we had to move down there to take shelter from Soviet attacks. Of course, being in the cellar brought back memories of fleeing down the steep staircase in our pajamas during air raids when we were much younger.

Judy and I climbed up on the pile of coal that we stored for the winter and began to level it off so that we could place mattresses on top of the coal if we had to sleep there. As we were digging around, Béla (back from Érd with Mother and Laci) came down to the cellar, telling us to come upstairs, right away. It turned out that the Austrian ambassador had called again with an urgent message reminding us that the very next day, November 4, we would need to meet the Red Cross convoy at eight a.m. for the trip to Austria. Judy and I stopped worrying about the coal cellar. Instead, we began thinking of what we wanted to take with us to Austria. With limited space in two suitcases for ten people, we were advised to wear in layers what would not fit in our suitcase. And, as pleasant as the October-November weather had been, we were reminded to not forget our winter coats.

My family went to bed in Aunt Lili's apartment at ten p.m., with me lying on a mattress on the living room floor. Everybody was happy that my mother and Laci were also with us.

At four a.m. the next morning, I woke up with a terrible feeling. I thought I was having a heart attack. My head was pounding, my heart was racing, and I did not know why. As I became more alert, I heard the steady, dull roar of Russian cannons as they approached Budapest. And this hellish sound became louder and louder. My mother heard the cannonade also. She did not know what to do. Should the family go down in the cellar, or should we attempt to meet the Red Cross convoy at Marczibányi Square? Mother and Aunt Ilike, in unison, decided: We must go ahead, even while the cannonade roared all around us.

So, on this fateful day, November 4, the two families said our good-byes to the rest of our relatives living at Béla Bartók Street 31. Neighbors were standing in the entranceways of their apartment houses looking at all of us hurrying past them. They yelled out to us, "Where are you running to? Don't you know the cannons are roaring? Go back, go back, and don't risk your lives!" But we no longer could listen. We had to march on.

With two bicycles, on which we had placed one suitcase for each family, the ten of us continued on our "historic journey." My mother and aunt, each with their four children, walked along Bartók Béla Street. We had to hurry. First, along the Danube under the rocky, towering protection of Gellért Hill, but then we had to cross over an open field under the Royal Castle, where perhaps we could be attacked by the approaching Russian military. As we were approaching Moscow Square, some seven kilometers from our home, we came very close to a pitched battle raging between the freedom fighters and the Soviet military. The bullets were flying in the air, with a typical "feeou, feeou" sound as they whizzed past us.

My mother found a shortcut so that we could avoid the shooting. "Everybody, right up on the hill, in the direction of Marczibányi Square," she said in her most forceful voice. With John and Béla propelling the suitcase-laden bikes, we made it to the Marczibányi Square location, huffing and puffing, as we climbed up the hill, arriving well before eight o'clock. We were totally exhausted. But, to our deepest shock and consternation, the Red Cross convoy was not there. It was gone. We had missed it! We had run as fast as we could, but all in vain!

The Crushing of the Revolution

Oh my God! What horrible news! The ten of us ran, ran, ran, uphill and down, just to reach the Red Cross convoy, and...now... it...is...gone! There is nobody at Marczibányi Square!

What to do now? Mother, always a person of leadership, declared, "Let's climb up these forty steps to the Austrian Embassy on Árvácska Street, on Rosehill. We will ask the Austrian ambassador for help." Well, up the hill we climbed. Every one of us was suffering and sweaty because we were wearing two layers of underwear, plus two wool sweaters, under our winter coats. Finally, the two families taking the serpentine road arrived at the pretty yellow neo-baroque villa that housed the Austrian Embassy.

Joseph Peinsipp, the ambassador himself, was on the balcony of the villa. He was in the process of taking down the red-white-red Austrian flag. He noticed our group below.

"Herr Gesandte," my mother yelled up to him in German. "We missed the convoy. What do we do now?"

"Well," the ambassador yelled back, "all of you, hurry and go back home."

"No, we can't—we won't," my mother put her foot down. She continued, "There is open fighting on Moscow Square. We absolutely cannot go back home. Please, please take us in!"

"Oh…then…well," Ambassador Peinsipp said, "All of you enter the villa at the service entrance behind the building. Our concierge and his wife just departed for Vienna. You can stay in their basement apartment."

"Oh, thank you," my mother responded. "We are going there right away."

And so we did. To our surprise, six other people were already there. These people apparently missed the convoy, just as we did. This underground apartment had one big bedroom (with the bed missing) and no furniture to sit on. There was a small breakfast nook, a smallish kitchen, and a tiny bathroom with a toilet. This was all the space there was for the sixteen of us.

The apartment was built into the side of Rosehill, so nobody had to worry about grenade attacks coming from the top of the hill. Everybody was quite safe. All of us had to sleep on the floor, wrapped in our winter coats. The two young girls, Judy and Lilla, slept on the U-shaped bench under the small breakfast table. Every morning when the girls woke up they were very sore because of the awkward position of the table's bench.

The Austrian ambassador had the courtesy to call Uncle Paul on the phone, telling him that the two mothers and eight children had missed the Red Cross convoy, but had found shelter at the Austrian Embassy. While we settled in, the fighting below in several areas of Budapest was going on with a terrible vengeance.

The Russian cannonade, which had awakened us that morning, was followed by the arrival of heavy armored vehicles on the main boulevards of the city. The barrage of gunfire could be heard, even from our distant location on Rosehill. The Russian military was ruthless in annihilating the strongholds of the freedom fighters—the barricades the rebels had constructed from the cobblestones of Budapest's sidewalks were no match for the Soviet troops. There was a fierce battle fought at the intersection of two main boulevards in Pest. The Russian tanks made mincemeat out of the five-story apartment buildings on the corner where Paul Maléter, now our ally, and his Hungarian units were still holding out at the military barracks near Corvin Köz.

Although both Csonka families were safe at the Austrian Embassy, we were very worried about the fate of the freedom fighters, who were risking their lives under the continued Soviet attack.

We learned that Ambassador Peinsipp had escaped to Vienna, leaving his personnel in charge of the embassy. There were some really wonderful, friendly employees, who looked in on us from time to time, bringing us bags of rice, and treating us to the most delicious Swiss chocolate bars—Tobler, Suchard, Milka, etc. When not eating chocolate, we ate everything else that had been left in the concierge's pantry.

In the evening, sister Judy, cousin Lilla, and I snuck upstairs and stepped out on the large terrace, overlooking the city in the valley. The Russian military lit up the evening sky over Budapest. Several large fires were burning, but we did not know whether it was the Budapest Opera House or St. Stephen's Basilica in Pest. What a terrible sight! What none of us suspected was that among the burning buildings was the government passport office, where the passports for both Csonka families were prepared, along with immigrant visas to the United States. All these documents were destroyed in the fire. (It took exactly three years before they were re-issued. Finally, on February 9, 1959, both Csonka families were in possession of immigrant passports to the United States, and we could finally leave for the free world.)

We stayed at the Austrian Embassy for twelve days. In the meantime, the weather turned to a very cold November. The employees of the Austrian Embassy briefed us about the terrible news that affected the whole country. The re-entering Soviet forces crushed "our" revolution. Many people died, many of them were very young, and many people were taken prisoner by the Russians. Many others left their homeland.

During the victorious days of the revolution, the land mines in the "no-men-zone" on the border between Austria and Hungary were detonated. The Hungarian border patrols no longer stopped people from fleeing the country. By December 1, thousands of Hungarians had left for Austria.

The actual fighting on the streets of Budapest was over by November 16. My mother and Aunt Ilike decided that it would be safe for us to return home. So, the mothers, Nelli and Ilike, and their children, John, Maria, Judy, and Laci; plus Béla, Melinda, Lilla, and Géza began the walk home. Totally distraught, with our heads bent down with grief, our procession walked home on the same route we had taken when we were desperately trying to reach the phantom convoy, some two weeks earlier.

The two families proceeded through the tunnel under the Royal Castle of Buda, some five kilometers away from the Austrian Embassy. On the other side of the tunnel, we came out to the banks of the Danube. To my great shock and dismay, I saw nothing but Russian tank after Russian tank on the Danube embankment all the way to Gellért Square, not far from our home. Next to each tank stood a Russian soldier with a machine gun in his hand, ready to shoot. These soldiers were short, stout, and with decidedly Mongolian features. Who knows whether they came from Kazakhstan or

Kyrgyzstan? These Russian soldiers, we were told, had been led to believe that they were in Berlin, fighting the monstrous Nazi regime of Hitler's successor.

Although they hoped we would be in Austria by now, Uncle Paul, Aunt Lili, and their families were glad to see us back home. Aunt Ilike's two tenants, young university students, had left the country for Austria. Now there was an extra room, which she offered to us. Yes! My mother finally saw the day when she was together with all her children. And, yes, I was deliriously happy because I had a mother again!

What happened to the Red Cross convoy that was supposed to take the Csonka families to Austria, one might ask. The other hopeful émigrés who arrived earlier than we did to Marczibányi Square on that fateful morning of November 4, 1956, were escorted to the Red Cross vehicles at seven a.m. Because of the anticipated Soviet attack, the convoy took off earlier than planned, at seven-fifteen a.m.

As the cars in the convoy were traveling to the border town of Hegyeshalom, between Hungary and Austria, a Russian unit intercepted the convoy. Everybody had to leave the cars. The Russian soldiers made everyone walk to a large ditch filled with water, near the road. Then, the people in the convoy were forced to stand in the water and sing the Hungarian national anthem. After this, the soldiers simply let everybody go. I guess, in retrospect, my family was lucky to have missed our ride with the Red Cross convoy.

Burying of Dreams and Reunion

The month of November 1956 became the saddest time period of Hungarian history. In his last message to the people of Hungary on Free Radio early in the morning of November 4, Imre Nagy, prime minister of the newly established Hungarian government, announced that Soviet forces had crushed the Hungarian Revolution. János Kádár, the Communist leader who was active in the pre-World War II political life of Hungary, became the chairman of the Council of Ministers of the People's Republic of Hungary, succeeding Imre Nagy on the fateful day of November 4, 1956.

Communist forces of the Kádár regime declared that the events of October 1956 were a "counter revolution." The Russian-backed Kádár government did everything to squelch the resistance of the Hungarian freedom fighters. The new Russian military presence in the country was painfully obvious in every aspect of civilian life. Young men were randomly captured by the Soviet military and placed on trains that took them to Siberia. Freedom of speech, the most powerful weapon of a truly democratic society, was brutally curtailed by the re-emerging Communist system. Several "plots" were discovered in which young people, organized by religious leaders, were severely punished by imprisonment.

Following a secret trial, Imre Nagy, Paul Maléter and others were executed in a prison in Romania on June 16, 1958, on charges of attempting to overthrow the Hungarian People's Republic. Cardinal József Mindszenty, who had been freed from eight years of Communist imprisonment during the revolution, now found shelter at the American Embassy in Budapest, but was unable to leave the embassy until 1971. Mindszenty, who personified uncompromising opposition to fascism and communism in Hungary, died in exile in Austria in 1975.

The atmosphere of Hungary became unbearable, again. Many young people decided to take the last chance to flee the country while the border to Austria was still open. These young people buried their dreams about a better life in Hungary and chose the uncertainty of immigration to a foreign country over the certainty of an oppressive political system in their homeland.

By December 5, my own two cousins, Paul Csonka and Béla Csonka, had made the decision to leave Hungary. They were both university students and of military age. They knew that if they did not leave the country then, they would perhaps never have the chance to go to the free world. Initially, because the political situation did not seem so dire to my brother John, age twenty-one at this time, he did not want to leave Hungary. He was surrounded by a group of friends who were very patriotic, still hoping for a better life in Hungary. But the moment the oppressive Kádár government was announced, these friends became disenchanted with the new system. They changed their minds, buried their dreams, and left Hungary, hopeless and dejected.

John had another reason for not wanting to leave Hungary. He was very much in love with Nicolette (Niki) D. from Budapest. Niki was seventeen years old. When John suggested to her that they should leave the country together, her parents opposed the plan. They thought that Niki, their only child, was much too young to flee into an unknown world. John was heartbroken.

When my mother learned that cousins Paul and Béla had left Hungary, she tried to persuade John to leave, too. She knew that John, being of military age, would never receive a passport and would never have the chance to see his father again. John, too, buried his dreams, and, reluctantly, took my mother's advice to leave.

So… on December 6, 1956, John said good-bye to his home and family. He traveled to Győr in western Hungary, where he stayed with the same relatives who helped my father leave Hungary back in 1948. John successfully crossed the Hungarian-Austrian border with the help of a guide.

On the very next day, December 7, John arrived at the Hungarian refugee camp outside of Vienna. By a lucky coincidence, he met Béla and Paul there. John and Béla arranged a meeting with the military commander of the refugee camp, and they explained to him that their respective fathers, living in Buffalo, New York, were U.S. citizens. Within two weeks, the three cousins received permission to board a U.S. military vessel, heading to New York. Paul, whose father and mother were Hungarian citizens and still in Budapest, was allowed to join his cousins because his godmother, Aunt Mária, sponsored him. She, like her brothers, was a U.S. citizen.

In January 1957, they arrived at Camp Kilmer in New Jersey. Nobody can imagine the joy of my father, Uncle

Béla, and Aunt Mária when they learned that their sons and nephew had made it to Vienna, and subsequently, that they had arrived in the United States. The two fathers and Aunt Mária rushed to Camp Kilmer to see Paul, John, and Béla, whom they had not seen for eight long years. This was a truly heartwarming reunion.

Arriving in the United States gave a terrific opportunity to the three young men to continue their college educations. Paul, age twenty-one, enrolled as a graduate student in nuclear physics at John Hopkins University in Baltimore, Maryland. He spoke English well and took advantage of a scholarship, which one of his father's friends secured for him. John and Béla, ages twenty-one and nineteen respectively, were college juniors at this time, and both enrolled as students at the University of Buffalo. John, who also spoke English, studied electrical engineering, while Béla took up mechanical engineering. Aunt Mária, who had left Hungary with her brothers in 1948, welcomed young John and young Béla with open arms to the Csonka home on Humboldt Parkway, in Buffalo.

Back in Budapest, my mother and Aunt Ilike rejoiced when they heard the news that their sons had arrived in the free world. Yet, the two mothers knew that their own lives would continue to be very difficult under the newly emerged Communist system. The big issue for both women was: what would happen to them and their three younger children in the new Kádár regime.

Later that December, in a quite desperate state, my mother plotted another escape from Hungary. She hoped that the border between Hungary and Yugoslavia would still be open, and we could flee that way, toward the south. She made initial preparations for our escape. She distributed the family's heirloom pieces among her three children. Her hope was that in Yugoslavia, we could sell the jewelry and make enough money for a temporary stay. (In preparation for the escape, I bought myself a pair of used ski boots I was going to wear if we had to walk across the border on rough terrain.)

Rumors circulated that units of Russian tanks had begun moving in near Baja, a border town in southern Hungary. Before taking all of us on the road, my mother decided to check out the escape route in person. She knew a certain pharmacist in Baja, whose two daughters were tenants in the fourth room of our apartment in Budapest. My mother planned to visit the pharmacist and ask his advice. When the bus she boarded to Baja was intercepted by ÁVO military, the soldiers asked her for the purpose of her trip, being suspicious of anyone who might be a potential "border crosser." My mother explained that she was going to visit a pharmacist, at a specified address. The ÁVO officers believed her and gave her free passage. What my mother learned from the pharmacist was that two days earlier the border had been sealed by Russian tanks. Now, nobody could escape Hungary through Yugoslavia. Once again, we were too late.

This was the sixth—and last—illegal attempt we made to flee Hungary. After this episode, there was nothing for my mother and aunt to do, but wait, wait, and wait, until the day immigration passports would be issued to both families, allowing them to leave the country legally. That wait lasted another two years.

At last, in January 1959, a magical moment happened. My mother and Aunt Ilike were informed by H.R., a Communist sympathizer of the Catholic clergy, that the Hungarian passport office had re-issued those immigration passports to the United States that had burned during the October 1956 events.

With the speed of a whirlwind, we packed our belongings and by February 5 we had shipped several crates of belongings to Buffalo, New York. There were tearful farewell parties with our friends, who already missed us and knew that they would never see us again.

The hardest thing to do was to say good-bye to my dear grandmother, Kornélia Simon, who at the time was over seventy years old. Next to her in our hearts stood our Aunt Lili, with Uncle Tamás and their eleven-year-old son, Tamás. It was heartbreaking to see the three of them crying as they gave us long farewell embraces at Keleti. We also said good-bye to Uncle Paul, Aunt Margó and their two daughters—our cousins Mazsi and Lívia—on the platform of the train that would be taking us to Vienna. Many dear friends and relatives came to the train station to say to us their farewells.

But, behind all the tearful good-byes and the sadness, there was the realization and the joy that the two Csonka families could, at last, leave behind an oppressive political regime. Above all, my mother and aunt rejoiced over the thought that our families would be reunited with our fathers, whom none of us had seen in eleven years. My mother and father, who had been thirty-eight and fifty-one years old respectively when my father left Hungary in 1948, would be forty-nine and sixty-two when they next saw each other.

The longed for reunion with my father, Uncle Béla, Aunt Mária, and the two young men, Béla and John, happened on June 16, 1959, at Idlewild Airport, in New York. What a great joy it was to have a whole family again!

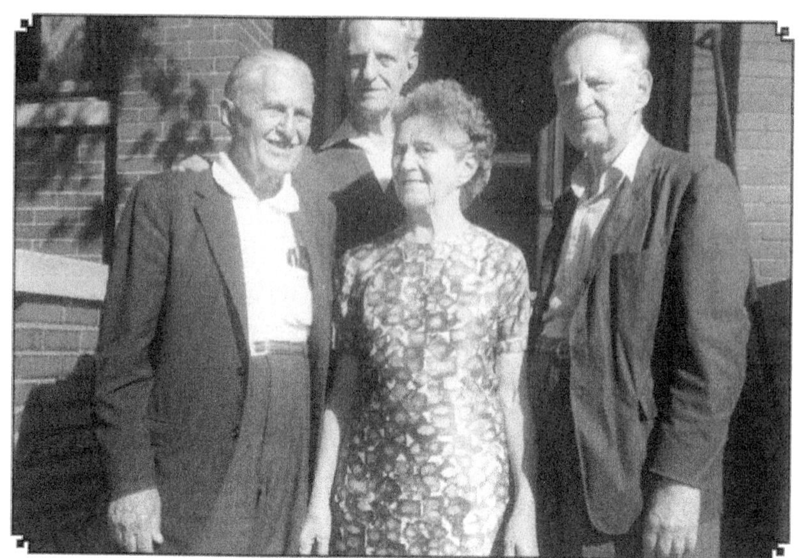

Buffalo reunion. Uncle Béla, Uncle Paul, Aunt Mária, and my father in front of my parent's home. Buffalo, New York, 1975

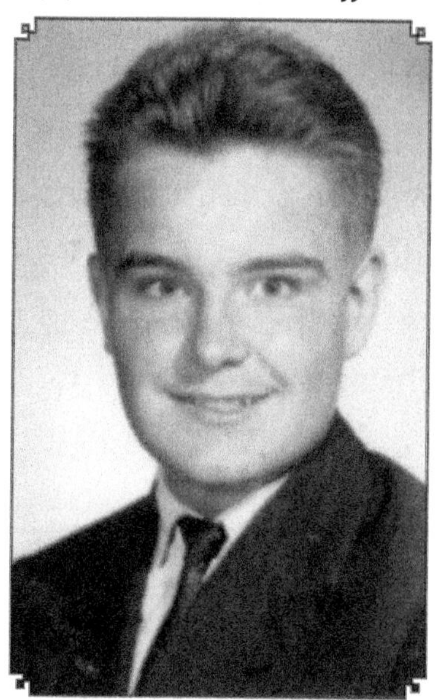

Laci, Cathedral Elementary School. Buffalo, 1961

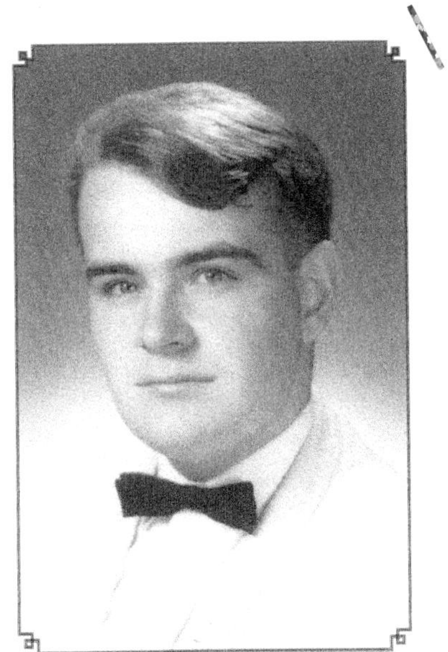

Laci, Canisius High School.
Buffalo, 1965

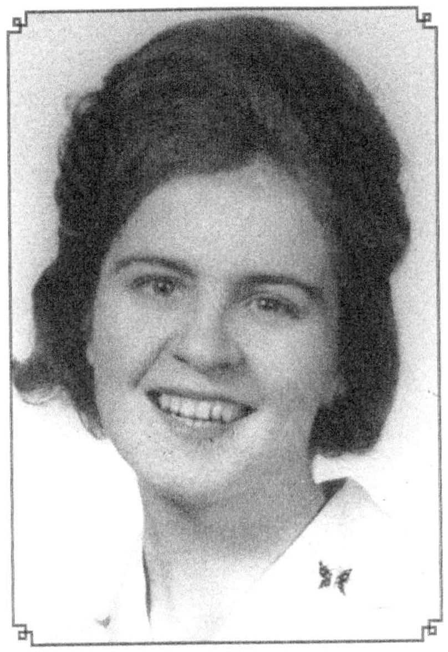

Judy, State University of
Buffalo. 1964

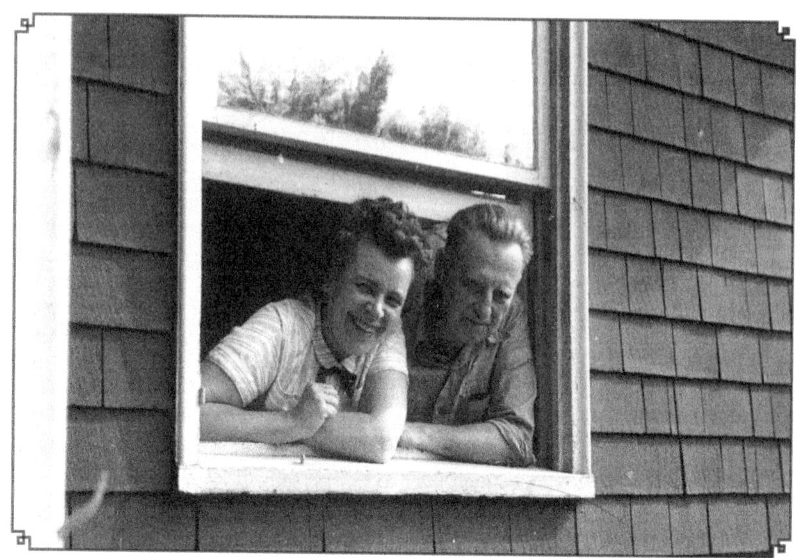

My parents, finally together. Buffalo, June 1959.

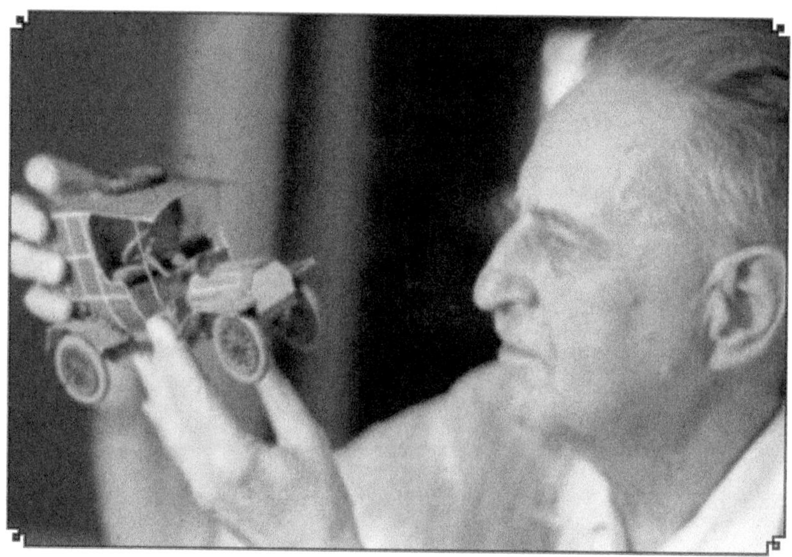

My father, John Csonka, with replica of the János Csonka postal vehicle. Buffalo, 1976

Epilogue

The years have come and gone. Great political forces shaped Hungarian history during the time period 1960 through 1980. With the fall of communism, a multiparty system emerged in 1988. In 1990, József Antall became the first democratically elected prime minister of the country. During Antall's brief tenure (1990–93), many individuals who were formerly persecuted by the Communist government were rehabilitated. Private properties were returned to their legal owners. János Csonka, my grandfather, whose name was erased from awareness in the Communist system, was re-discovered, and honored by the Hungarian media.

Even the Csonka Machine Factory, whose name was changed to Small Engine and Machine Factory by the Communist government, received back its original name. Today, a statue of János Csonka, inventor, stands in a small park at 44 Fehérvári Street, Budapest, adjacent to the original plant that he envisioned.

Let us take a moment to trace the lives of the eleven Csonka cousins who reached adulthood. It is actually very sad that nine of the eleven were forced to leave their homeland because of political oppression. The only two cousins who remained in Budapest were Margit (Mazsi) and Lívia, daughters of Uncle Paul and his wife Margó, who likewise stayed in Hungary.

The three older Csonka cousins, Paul, John, and Béla, established successful careers in the United States. Cousin Paul has been a professor of theoretical physics at the University of Oregon since 1968. During this time he worked at several universities and laboratories both in the U.S. and in Europe, including the international CERN laboratory in Geneva, Switzerland. Paul is married, lives in Eugene, Oregon, and has raised a family of three children. He has three granddaughters.

John Csonka worked at the Westinghouse plant in Buffalo, beginning in 1960. He held a master's degree in computer technology. To the greatest sorrow of his entire family, John died in a skiing accident at age thirty-one in South Buffalo in January 1967. His upward-arching career was cut short by this tragic accident.

Béla Csonka Jr. became a successful mechanical engineer. He married in 1965 and raised a family of three children. He had three grandchildren. He attained a managerial position with the Ariens Company in Green Bay, Wisconsin. Béla died of heart failure in Arizona.

The two younger Csonka boys, Géza and László (Laci), have grown into mature adulthood. Géza Csonka lives in Kenmore, N.Y., with his wife and son. His two daughters and two granddaughters reside in Ithaca, N.Y. Géza managed the engineering department for the Osmose company.

László Csonka is a professor of microbiology at Purdue University in West Lafayette, Indiana. He gives lectures in his field and travels internationally. My younger brother is married and has two children, one of whom is Susan Antonia Csonka.

The group of three younger Csonka girls, Lívia, Judy, and Lilla, are all married. Lívia is an English teacher and lives in Budapest. She has eleven grandchildren. She spent many years developing the János Csonka Museum in the basement of the apartment house originally owned by my grandfather.

My sister Judy lives with her husband and two of her children in New Jersey, with another daughter living in North Carolina. Judy worked as a medical technologist in the United States and Switzerland. She has eight grandchildren.

Lilla lives with her husband in Cary, North Carolina. For many years she worked as a chemist in Boston, Palo Alto, and Kansas City. She has two sons and four grandchildren.

Of the three older Csonka girls, I am the only one still living. My cousin Mazsi died of cancer in 2001 at an age of sixty-three years. She also remained in Budapest, where she was a teacher of English and Arabic. She was married and lived with her husband and son. My cousin Melinda died just recently of pneumonia at age seventy-six in Buffalo. Melinda, who was born with a disability, managed to function in a controlled environment. She married in 1970, but had lived alone since her divorce in 1976. Melinda had a great love of people and enjoyed classical music.

And now, we come to Maria Csonka Bardos, the oldest of the Csonka girls. As the author of this book, I would like to tell you about myself. I was born March 10, 1938, in Budapest, Hungary, at the time of the Anschluss. Following a happy childhood, I experienced the terrors of World War II and survived a near fatal explosion.

After finishing my schooling in Budapest in 1957, I was denied entry to the University of Budapest for study of the English language. In September that year

I enrolled in a two-year foreign trade correspondent training school program in English and German.

Once in the United States, I began my college studies at the University of Buffalo, majoring in German with a minor in Spanish. I graduated, cum laude, with a bachelor of arts degree in 1962 and was elected to join the Phi Beta Kappa society. I continued my studies at the State University of New York at Buffalo, receiving a doctorate in German literature and linguistics in 1970.

In December 1967, I married László Farnek in Buffalo. He was a former deportee from Mezőberény whom I met in 1951. Our marriage ended in a divorce in 1979. After a four-year teaching career at the University of Buffalo (1965-69), I began a twenty-six year teaching career at Amherst Junior High School, Amherst, New York. With state certification in three languages, I taught German, Spanish, and Latin. Following retirement in 1995, I taught on a part-time basis in small local colleges.

My parents, John and Nelli Csonka, moved from downtown Buffalo to Williamsville, a suburb of Buffalo, and it was there that my father died of lung cancer at the age of eighty-two in 1980. I, while teaching in the Amherst school system, bought a home close to my mother and lived there for twenty-two years. In 1994 my mother, who had lived alone since my father's death and had serious health issues, moved to her daughter Judy's home in New Jersey and died two years later at the age of eighty-six.

When I was teaching part-time after retirement, I met Dr. Thomas Bardos, a Hungarian medicinal chemist, who was introduced to me by mutual friends. Tom was from Budapest and twenty-two years my senior. He and I found lots of common elements in our family backgrounds and in our cultural orientation. We were married in December 2002. I sold my home and joined him at Canterbury Woods, a continuing care retirement community in Williamsville. Here we lived, happily, for almost ten years. We enjoyed a wonderful life together until he died in May 2012.

Since 2004 I have been teaching various courses for senior citizens at "Canterbury University." These courses include world literature, Russian literature, and Greek and Roman mythology; I just completed teaching a class on Leonardo da Vinci and the Italian High Renaissance.

Now that I have introduced myself, I would like to tell you the reasons why I wrote this book, which focuses on my early life. It describes the horror of World War II and the emergence of the communist form of government in Hungary. The narrative zeroes in on my own family and pays special attention to our deportation during 1951–53. The final section of the book highlights the political events that led up to the Hungarian Revolution of 1956 and describes the moments of a happy reunion with my father in 1959.

I decided to write this account for the youngest generation of the Csonka family, those descendants who have all been born in the United States, and, therefore, had no direct experience with the events happening in Hungary during the years 1943–59. My goal was to draw a picture of the innumerable obstacles the older generation had to overcome to survive the terrors of war and political oppression. My hope is that my nieces, nephews, grandnieces, and grandnephews will better understand the challenges and difficulties my parents and their grandparents faced in Hungary during the time of historic events that shook the world.

Family Trees

Csonka Family Tree

János Csonka 1852–1939
and
Johanna Winkler 1864–1946

I. **Pál (Paul) 1896–1988 m. Margit (Margó) Warga 1910–2009**
- **Paul Jr. 1935–** m. Márti Gombos
    - *Emese 1978 m. Daniel Parker
        - ~Kinga 2012
        - ~Ilona 2013
        - ~Emese 2016
    - *Paul 1979
    - * Lívia 1983 m. Scott Perry
- **Margit (Mazsi) 1938–2001** m. István Rombay
    - *András 1974
- **Lívia 1940–** m. Alajos Stróbl
    - *Katalin 1966–2014 m. Balázs Lengyel
        - ~Domokos 1995
        - ~Mariann 1996
        - ~Miklós 1999
        - ~Paul 2007
    - *Kristóf 1968 m. Bea Kisdi
        - ~Anna 1996
        - ~Dániel 1998
        - ~Tamás 2001
        - ~Levente 2005
    - *Erzsébet 1970 m. András Gianone
        - ~Kinga
        - ~Ágoston
        - ~ János

roman numeral	children of Csonka-Winkler and Simon-Pintér
•	grandchildren
*	great grandchildren
~	great great grandchildren
m.	married
d.	divorced

II. János (John) 1897–1980 m. Kornélia (Nelli) Simon 1910–1996

- **John Jr. 1935–1967**
- **Maria 1938–** m. (1) László Farnek – d.,
  (2) Thomas Bardos 1915-2012
- **Judit (Judy) 1941–** m. Peter Novak 1935
  *Nicolette 1971 m. Michael Hommer
  ~Alexandra 1992
  ~Brandon 1992
  ~Christina 1994
  ~Daniel 1994
  *Andrea 1973 m. Michael Baer
  ~Sarah 2003
  ~Nathan 2006
  *Peter 1973 m. Lisa Wigginton
  ~Matthew 2005
  ~Brian 2007
- **László (Laci) 1947–** m. Carol Lindquist
  *Nicolas 1985
  *Susan 1987

III. Ilona (Ilonka) 1898–1939 m. János Feyér

- Iluska 1927–1940

IV. Béla 1900–1990 m. Ilona (Ili, Ilike) Wotzasik 1913–1994

- **Béla Jr. 1937–2008** m. Sharron Reilly
  *Lisa 1961 m. Gary Foltz
  ~Savannah 2002
  ~Peyton 2004
  ~Alex 2010
  *John 1969
  *Steven 1978
- **Melinda 1938–2014** m. Daniel Boland – d.

- **Lilla 1942–** m. Raja Khalifah
  *Peter 1974 m. Surita Baktia
  ~Julian 2006
  ~Evan 2009
  *Anthony 1977 m. Sonia
  ~Hana 2013
  ~Thomas 2015
- **Géza 1946–** m. Judy Hurd
  *Susan 1975 m. Anesti Zakos – d.
  ~Cecilia 2004
  ~Liliana 2008
  *Michelle 1977
  *Paul 1981 m. Jen Len

V. Mária 1901–1995

Simon Family Tree

Károly Simon 1883–1943
and
Kornélia Pintér 1887–1970

I. Kornélia (Nelli) 1910–1996 m. János (John) Csonka 1897–1980

- **John Jr. 1935–1967**
- **Maria 1938–** m. (1) László Farnek – d.,
  (2) Thomas Bardos 1915-2012
- **Judit (Judy) 1941–** m. Peter Novak
  *Nicolette 1971 m. Michael Hommer
  ~Alexandra 1992
  ~Brandon 1992
  ~Christina 1994
  ~Daniel 1994
  *Andrea 1973 m. Michael Baer
  ~Sarah 2003
  ~Nathan 2006
  *Peter 1973 m. Lisa Wigginton
  ~Matthew
  ~Brian
- **László (Laci) 1947–** m. Carol Lindquist
  *Nicolas 1985
  *Susan 1987

II. Erzsébet (Lili) 1911–1984 m. Tamás Vidóczy

- **Tamás Vidóczy Jr. 1948–** m. Andrea Vendel
  *Katalin 1978
  *Judith 1981 m. Ákos Monspart
  ~Martin 2008
  ~Matthew 2012
  ~Ágost 2015
  ~Botond 2015

Author's Note

I have dedicated this book to my niece, Susan Antonia Csonka of West Lafayette, Indiana, for her willingness to ask questions about the Csonka family history.

Many thanks go to Reed Taylor of Williamsville, New York, for encouraging me to start writing my life story. I would like to recognize my cousin Tamás Vidóczy of Budapest, Hungary, for his comments on the initial chapters of my book. Special thanks go to Carol Lederman, Marilyn Rodwin, and Shirley Rosenthal at Canterbury Woods for their first reading of my manuscript. The enthusiasm and support of my friend Carol Kuhn helped me throughout the writing.

I am grateful also to Ágota Sántha, who spent many hours putting into type my handwritten manuscript.

Finally, I would like to express my appreciation to my editor, Anne Crookall Hockenos, for her invaluable comments, without which my book would not have become a reality.

Note: *A spelling curiosity: the last name of my great-grandfather, Vince Tsonka, reflects old Hungarian orthography. By the time my grandfather was born in 1852, the spelling of the last name was modernized to Csonka. My family kept this modernized spelling.*

CPSIA information can be obtained
at www.ICGtesting.com
Printed in the USA
BVOW11s2146121116
467651BV00003B/4/P